BETTER FEEDBACK, IMPROVED LESSONS

BETTER FEEDBACK, IMPROVED LESSONS

A How-To Guide for Principals, Teacher Educators, and Mentors

Jacqueline G. Van Schooneveld

ROWMAN & LITTLEFIELD
Lanham • Boulder • New York • London

Published by Rowman & Littlefield
A wholly owned subsidiary of The Rowman & Littlefield Publishing Group, Inc.
4501 Forbes Boulevard, Suite 200, Lanham, Maryland 20706
www.rowman.com

Unit A, Whitacre Mews, 26-34 Stannary Street, London SE11 4AB

British Library Cataloguing in Publication Information Available

Library of Congress Cataloging-in-Publication Data Available

ISBN 978-1-4758-3578-6 (cloth : alk. paper)
ISBN 978-1-4758-3579-3 (pbk. : alk. paper)

∞™ The paper used in this publication meets the minimum requirements of American National Standard for Information Sciences—Permanence of Paper for Printed Library Materials, ANSI/NISO Z39.48-1992.

Printed in the United States of America

CONTENTS

ACKNOWLEDGMENTS

Throughout my life, I have been fortunate to travel around the world and visit a range of school communities. I have seen one-room schoolhouses full of students singing and dancing in the townships of Cape Town, South Africa. I have witnessed students in dirt-floor classrooms in rural Costa Rica get excited to demonstrate their ability to communicate in both Spanish and English. I have watched students in China perform self-created presentations to represent their culture. I have worked with students in the United States in rural, suburban, and urban settings, and seen students in public, charter, and private schools engage in exploratory lessons that bring content to life. All these amazing experiences have been the result of passionate teachers who just want to spark students' love for learning.

The two people who have inspired me most to write this book have been my son Jameson and daughter Olivia. Every day, Jameson and Olivia ask me questions about the things they see, hear, and experience. They want answers. I want them to have teachers who don't tell them why, but engage them in finding the answers themselves. I want them to have school experiences I have been privileged to observe around the world and throughout the country. I want them to have teachers who are confident in creating lessons that make content come to life.

While I have witnessed and collaborated with some of the most amazing educators, I have experienced teachers who did not believe in my own abilities. Teachers who told my parents I was not smart. This book would not have been possible without my parents, Howard and Frances Flicker, who never listened to those teachers. They believed that I could do or be anything I wanted. They were the first people to develop my love for learning. They encouraged me to excel in school.

Throughout my professional and personal life, I have been fortunate to have people who have supported me. My brothers Benjamin and Robert have been my cheerleaders through life. My friends have been some of my best traveling companions and have challenged me to think in different ways and see the world through different lenses. The teachers and administrators at Mott Hall II gave me the space to develop my practice and provided support and guidance. The amazing teachers at Cherry Creek School District were incredible teacher role models. The professors at Bucknell University, Columbia University, and the University of Pennsylvania developed my content but also challenged my perceptions of what it means to educate. The students and faculty at West Chester University challenge me to think of new methods to support future teachers. Finally, I would like to thank my husband, Andrew, who has supported me throughout this process. This book was only possible because of these wonderful friends, family, and colleagues.

The book represents my passion for working with teachers, administrators, teacher educators, and aspiring teachers to provide support systems that can enable educators to feel confident in creating engaging lessons. My goal is not to create teachers who all teach the same way. Instead, it is my aim to create educators who want to design classrooms and school communities that have students learning and developing a love for school. I want my kids, and all children, to have these types of teachers and learning experiences.

BOOK OVERVIEW

This book is intended to be used by supervisors (principal, cooperative teacher, mentor teacher, teacher educator, etc.). Supervisors will learn different strategies for providing written and oral feedback to teachers regarding their lesson plans. Chapters 2, 3, and 4 provide the rationale for each strategy, a description for each strategy, and suggestions for implementation.

After reading the different strategies, a supervisor might suggest to his/her mentee(s) (teacher, novice teacher, student teacher, field student, etc.) to read some of the strategies the supervisor might want to use. This is not required; however, it would provide good information to the mentee and allow him/her to know what to expect from the supervisor.

Chapter 5 is written for both the supervisor *and* mentee. Before using any of the strategies described in the book, both the supervisor and mentee need a common language. Using the case studies described in the final chapter will build a dialog around the purpose of lesson planning and discuss how they will work together to use these different strategies.

This book may be used by a supervisor just wanting to improve their supervision practices. It does not need to be read with a specific mentee in mind or with a specific situation that needs to be addressed. Any supervisor can read the chapters about strategies and apply these practices.

This is not a book for supervisors who want a quick fix. This book is intended for supervisors who want to work with teachers using their lesson plans to be effective leaders in their classroom and at their school.

1

RATIONALE FOR LESSON PLANNING

ARE WE DEVELOPING CHEFS OR SOUS CHEFS?

The head chef of an elite restaurant has familiarity and expertise in creating a superior dining experience—from the ambiance to the finely constructed dishes. The chef might have worked countless hours to develop a perfect dish. Once the chef has polished the dish, he/she passes the recipe to the sous chefs to practice and reconstruct that specific dish over and over again.

If supervisors (principals, head teachers, mentors, cooperative teachers, teacher educators, etc.) have experience and expertise creating lessons, why not just give novice teachers or struggling teachers the perfect lesson plan to reproduce? Isn't that what a top chef would do?

A supervisor can pass along great lesson plans; however, the goal of supervising novice and struggling teachers through lesson plans is not to develop sous chefs. This book is intended to provide supervisors with specific tools and strategies for providing feedback on lesson plans that will help develop competent teachers. Teachers need support and guidance on what to think about in terms of content, pedagogy, and classroom management.

The rest of this chapter provides the research for using lesson plans as an educational tool for teachers. The research gives the rationale for why it is necessary to have different strategies and methods for providing meaningful feedback on teachers' lesson plans. There is also a section dedicated to what counts as a lesson plan and specific items that supervisors should look for in a lesson plan. Finally, there is a brief overview of the following chapters.

RESEARCH TO SUPPORT LESSON PLANNING

Teaching has three components: (1) teacher knowledge, (2) classroom instruction, and (3) instructional design practices.

Historically, teacher knowledge was what a teacher knew about a specific subject area. For instance, a chemistry teacher would need to know the periodic table. Educational researchers expanded this idea, suggesting that knowing content was not enough. A teacher would need to know the content, how to communicate the content, and how to engage students in meaningful activities (Shulman, 1986, 1987). For example, students would not memorize the periodic table. Instead, they would work in labs to identify elements, based on characteristics associated with that element. To do that, a teacher would need an in-depth understanding of the content and know pedagogical practices associated with that content that would be developmentally appropriate for students.

The second component, classroom instruction, is everything the teacher does during class time. This includes the interactions a teacher has with students, the application of curriculum materials, and the use of resources (e.g., technology, manipulatives, worksheets, etc.) (Wenglinsky, 2000).

Most strategies for supervision are directly connected to classroom instruction. The most common is when a supervisor watches instruction and conferences with the teacher afterward to provide feedback about what he/she observed. Other times, a supervisor will pre-conference to discuss what will happen during instruction, then watch instruction, and then post-conference to discuss what they observed during the lesson. A third strategy is when a supervisor provides in-the-moment feedback during instruction that the teacher can apply immediately. All three types are forms of clinical supervision that are beneficial, but focus *purely* on instruction (Gall and Acheson, 2011).

The final component is instructional design practices. These encompass a range of teaching activities that take place outside of the classroom to prepare for instruction (Van Schooneveld, 2014). These practices include professional development (Garet et al., 2001), collaborating with colleagues (Lieberman, 2009; Wood, 2007), exploring curriculum materials (Grossman and Thompson, 2008; Remillard, 2000), and lesson planning (Li, Chen, and Kulm, 2009; Smith, Bill, and Hughes, 2008).

Lesson planning is a unique type of instructional design practice for two reasons. First, it is an instructional design practice in which most, if not all, teachers have received some type of formal training in their teacher education or certification programs (Kagan and Tippins, 1992; Zazkis, Liljedahl, and Sinclair, 2009). Second, lesson planning is the first representation of a teacher's thoughts about what good instruction of the content should be (Lampert, 2001).

According to Li, Chen, and Kulm (2009), "If teachers can design well-thought-out and high-quality lesson plans, as a process of curriculum plans at the micro-level, they build a solid base for classroom implementation" (p. 717). Lesson planning can be an educative tool for teachers if they use it to develop their content, think about pedagogical strategies, and anticipate how students should act during class time. If used in this manner, lesson planning has a high potential to impact teachers' instruction.

In an exploratory study that examined novice teachers' mathematical knowledge for teaching (Ball, Thames, and Phelps, 2008) and patterns associated to their lesson plans, there were two findings that support using lesson plans as a vehicle for supervision (Van Schooneveld, 2014).

This study showed that teachers who had evidence of higher cognitive-demand activities or a variety of cognitive-demand activities written in their lesson plans performed higher on the Mathematical Knowledge for Teaching (MKT) assessment (LMT, 2007) than teachers who did not include that information in their written lesson plans (Van Schooneveld, 2014). This finding suggests lesson plans that include content and pedagogical practices of a high cognitive level came from teachers who understood the content. This finding does not mean teachers must know the content before writing the lesson.

Writing a lesson plan should be a space for teachers to build content and pedagogical understanding. Teachers cannot know everything, but by going through the process of lesson planning, they must think about the content, pedagogical practices, resources available, and so on. A teacher can develop his/her knowledge base through planning.

Teachers with a higher knowledge base create better lesson plans. Although the study did not examine the execution of those lesson plans, someone could predict that a teacher who created higher cognitive-demand lessons, and performed higher on a content assessment, has a higher potential for communicating content and responding to students' academic needs during instructional time.

Another key finding from the study showed that teachers who wrote lesson plans that had no variety in instruction (i.e., all lecture based), or unclear structure as to how class time would be organized, scored the lowest on the MKT assessment. The plans of teachers who scored the highest on the assessment had a very clear structure. Those teachers wrote that they would start as a whole class and end with independent work. The middle section of the lessons had a range of activities that would engage students (hands-on activities, discussions, modeling, etc.) in ways that aligned to the content being taught (Van Schooneveld, 2014).

Teachers who understood the content wrote lesson plans that demonstrated understanding of how to engage students, and they thought through the sequence of instructional time. This study did not examine how teachers *taught* the lesson; however, the study suggested there would be higher potential for what could happen during instructional time from teachers who thought through organization of the lesson and developed a variety of activities, as opposed to teachers who did not.

The two findings linking teachers' content and pedagogical knowledge to their written lesson plans provide evidence for why lesson plans could be used as an educative tool to build teachers' content and pedagogical practices. This form of instructional design practice, in which all teachers learn and practice, has potential for what could happen during instructional time. Why should supervisors wait until instruction to provide supervision and mentoring when lesson planning can be an educative tool to develop teachers' practices?

What Counts as a Lesson Plan?

There are different formats for lesson plans and different ways teachers create their lessons (Hunter, 1994; McCutcheon, 1980; Thornbury,

1999). Studies have shown that teachers' lesson plans change based on teaching experience (Li, Chen and Kulm, 2009). "This is not because lesson plans become less important; rather, experienced teachers have internalized the lesson planning process" (Johnson, 2000, p. 73). A novice teacher's lessons will look different from those of teachers who have taught for ten years. Experienced teachers who are reassigned to a new grade level or a new subject area might have more detailed lesson plans than teachers with the same years of experience but teaching the same grade or subject.

Recently, there have been alternative approaches to combat the traditional lesson plan formats (John, 2006). One model has been lesson plays (Zazkis, Liljedahl and Sinclair, 2009) in which teachers extract a part of their lesson plan and write out the dialog (a play) they imagine taking place during that portion of the lesson.

In Japan, teachers engage in "lesson studies" (Fernandez, Cannon and Chokshi, 2003). Teachers work together in learning teams to critically review a lesson and examine the content. They are challenged to think about the content and different approaches for how students can understand the content and learn the information. Teachers are expected to apply what they developed during the lesson study to their own instruction.

Regardless of which approach is used, there are common things teachers think through when constructing a lesson plan. These domains of a lesson plan include (1) treatment of content in the lesson, (2) consideration of students' learning needs, (3) acknowledgment of influencing factors, and (4) structure and organization of the lesson plan aligned to instruction (Van Schooneveld, 2014).

Treatment of Content

Teachers' treatment of the content is where a teacher provides evidence that he/she understands the content. For example, in a literacy class the teacher might include vocabulary words and definitions. A math teacher might include possible math problems or word problems that represent the mathematical skill or concept being taught. A social studies teacher might include relevant historical dates. These are just examples of how teachers could provide evidence that they understand the content.

Content knowledge can also be viewed through the activities a teacher constructs. For example, a science teacher could prove he/she knows the content by writing a lesson that includes a descriptive science lab in which students participate in an experiment that would have them explore and understand a science concept. A teacher's lesson plan that includes a learning activity in which students gain content knowledge through their participation is another way a teacher might demonstrate content understanding.

Consideration of Students' Learning Needs

Evidence of considering students' learning needs is the second domain in lesson plans. This comes in multiple forms, most commonly through assessments, differentiation, modifications, and/or accommodations. This can also be seen in the variety of activities a teacher creates. For example, a teacher could use centers and connect each center to a different multiple intelligence. Any representation in a lesson plan that shows a teacher has thought about different types of learners and ways to meet a diverse group of learners would be evidence that a teacher has thought about his/her students.

Acknowledgment of Influencing Factors

It is important to be able to identify in lesson plans the external factors that influence how and/or what an educator teaches. For example, most lesson plans include state standards. The standards are external factors impacting what a teacher does. Another example would be the use of a school textbook. The text would have been selected by the school board or committee and expected to be used by teachers. Schools and/or districts might have requirements for what is included in formal lesson plans. Those items become external factors impacting a teacher. Most of these items are unconsciously included in teachers' lesson plans.

Structure and Organization of the Lesson Plan Aligned to Instruction

Structure, organization, and format used in writing the lesson plan and in thinking about how instructional time will be used is the final domain. Does a teacher have specific items identified in the lesson plan (i.e., standards, learning objectives, procedures, assessments, etc.)? As mentioned earlier, the format might be evidence of external factors if it is linked to a school, district, or teacher education program. Regardless, there should be a clear format that communicates a teacher's understanding of items to include in his/her written plans.

The lesson plan must also convey the organization and structure of how the teacher plans to deliver the lesson during instructional time. Is there a clear way the teacher opens the lesson and concludes the lesson? Does the teacher think about time management and how much time students will spend on an activity? Does the teacher think about transitions for students between activities, and making connections between the activities and the content? Evidence of how teachers organize and structure the lesson provides a window into what their instruction might look like.

These four domains of lesson plans can look completely different for all teachers. However, good lesson plans will document each of these four domains (Van Schooneveld, 2014). This book does not provide a format or dictate how teachers should write their lesson plans but works under the assumption that lesson plans must include evidence of each of these four domains.

Addressing the Critics

Although lesson plans can reveal teachers' initial thoughts about instruction, there is opposition for using lesson plans, which is important to understand and address. Critics have made the argument that what is created in the lesson plan is not always enacted (Stein, Grover, and Henningsen, 1996). Even though lesson plans cannot fully predict what teachers will do during instruction, lesson plans can provide evidence about how teachers think about the content, students, and other variables before instruction. The ways teachers think about these components of teaching before instruction provide the basic building blocks for what can happen during instruction.

Other skeptics believe that lesson plans that are enacted paralyze a teacher's ability to be flexible and adapt to different situations in the classroom (Zahorik, 1970; Zazkis, Liljedahl, and Sinclair, 2009). Novice teachers who are nervous often rely on their lesson plans, and sometimes script out their lessons. Unfortunately, those plans become crutches. Teachers in this predicament cannot be stripped of their lesson plans but, instead, need guidance for how to adapt those lesson plans to be educative tools and not hindrances. This is even more of a rationale for providing supervision on lesson plans.

2

PROVIDING WRITTEN FEEDBACK ON LESSON PLANS

Regardless of your position (principal, colleague, supervisor, or cooperative teacher), you might be required to provide written feedback on a lesson plan. There are different rationales for when to provide the feedback and strategies for how to provide the feedback. In this chapter, you'll learn the rationale, strategies, benefits, drawbacks, and tips for providing written feedback on lesson plans *prior to instruction*.

RATIONALE FOR PROVIDING WRITTEN FEEDBACK

The goal of providing written feedback on lesson plans prior to instruction is to give teachers or prospective teachers opportunities to reflect on the content and methodologies and make modifications *before* they interact with students. Oftentimes, a teacher's lesson plan is their first thought about what good content instruction should be (Lampert, 2001). Providing written feedback on the lesson plan prior to instruction gives a teacher at least two opportunities to think through the instruction and content: once while writing the lesson plan and again by reflecting on the feedback and making modifications to the lesson plan. Although what is created in the lesson plan might not be *exactly* what is carried out in the classroom (Stein, Grover, and Henningsen, 1996), being forced to think through the content and instruction multiple times can only better prepare the teacher.

For this reason, providing written feedback that engages a teacher in the reflective practice is important. Just writing evaluative language on a lesson plan (e.g., *good*, *back*, *right*, *wrong*, *okay*, etc.) does not *engage* the teacher. Therefore, there are two strategies for providing written feedback to engage the teacher. Both strategies require the teacher to reflect on the written feedback and make changes to his/her lesson plan before implementing it in the classroom.

For either of these strategies to be beneficial, the teacher must *actively* engage by changing the lesson plan. Requiring the teacher to do something with the written feedback not only impacts that specific lesson, but also impacts his/her ability to take that feedback and transfer those suggestions to future lesson plans. The goal is to improve the current lesson and how a teacher thinks about lesson planning.

Strategy 1: *Providing Stems*

Providing Stems is a strategy that is typically used for novice teachers or teachers who are teaching in a new content or grade level. Stems are designed to provide initial teacher talk that can shape teachers' instructional delivery throughout the lesson. It is important to remember it is a learning tool.

What is a stem? A stem is an incomplete statement. A lesson plan is composed of many statements in the introduction, procedure, and closing sections. For example, a *full statement* might be:

> *To begin today's lesson I want you to reflect on yesterday's lesson, which introduced Shakespeare's* Romeo and Juliet, *and write down a quote from yesterday's reading that you think demonstrates personification.*

The statement is a full idea. These can take place in the introduction, procedure, or closing sections of the lesson plan.

The goal behind *Providing Stems* is to teach teachers how to write these types of statements by engaging them in the processes of constructing them. For this reason, *the supervisor should only provide the stem, and not the full statement.* In the example above, the stem is

> To begin today's lesson I want you to reflect on yesterday's lesson, which introduced Shakespeare's *Romeo and Juliet*, and . . . .

The stem sets the stage, but pushes the teacher to think about what he/she wants the students to do. By providing the stem, the teacher must reflect on the information and think about how to complete the statement. The teacher becomes an active participant in rethinking the lesson.

If the stem is given as a complete statement, the teacher will just take the statement, but not be responsible for constructing it. The goal is to teach a teacher how to construct and infuse stems into his/her lesson and eventually do it without being prompted or given the statement.

Depending on the part of the lesson plan, the stem will look different. In the following subsections, you'll see the goals and examples of *Providing Stems* at the beginning, procedure, and concluding sections of the lesson.

Stems at the Beginning Section of a Lesson Plan

Stems can be used at the beginning of a lesson plan for teachers to rethink what the first couple of minutes of class time should look like. Often times, teachers jump right into the lesson, or use the beginning of instructional time to take care of logistical issues (e.g., attendance, homework, etc.).

The purpose of the stem at the beginning of the lesson is to force a teacher to rethink how he/she is introducing the lesson, and how to motivate students through a quick activity that introduces (or reviews) content that will connect to the lesson.

Before a supervisor can think about constructing a stem, it is important to think first about the full statement. The following is an example of a *full statement* for the beginning of a lesson plan:

> To begin the lesson, I would like you to write down two different math word problems that you think represent the addition problem 5 + 7.

The statement has three parts. The first part acknowledges *when* in the lesson the activity takes place. For an experienced teacher it might not be needed, but it helps a novice teacher to think about the sequence of the lesson. A supervisor could be even more specific and include whether students are reflecting on previously taught material, or if it is something new. For example: "To begin the lesson I want you to refer back to yesterday's lesson on word problems."

The second key element of each statement includes direct instructions *about what will be produced.* From this example, students will write two math word problems. It is clear and specific. This helps students know what is expected of them. It also helps novice teachers think about what they want produced, gives clear directions, and avoids ambiguity when students are asked to do something.

Finally, the statement focuses on *content*. In this case, students must use their understanding of addition and word problems. Teachers can get caught up in the activity and lose sight of the content that needs to be covered. That is why it is important for these statements to have a clear content focus.

For the introduction of a lesson, the statement could have content that is a review of a previous lesson or require students to think about new content that will be covered. Either way, the statement requires students to think about content that will lead into the lesson. The rule for statements written for the beginning portion of the lesson is that the teacher must have the students think about the content and produce something.

When providing written feedback, the supervisor should provide one or two of the key elements of the statement and ask the teacher to develop the remaining part, which is what makes it a stem and not a full statement. The teacher needs to participate in the construction of the statement.

Since there are two goals associated with the introductory portion of the lesson, the stem should only provide one of those goals already intact. In other words, a supervisor might provide the *content* and ask the teacher to think about what the students would need to *produce*. For instance, in a biology class, a lesson about mammals could have an introductory stem that reads as follows:

> *To begin today's lesson, there are 10 pictures of different animals on the board that include mammals, birds, insects and amphibians. I want each of you to . . .*

In this stem, the supervisor identified where in the lesson the stem took place and included the content. The supervisor left out what needed to be produced, allowing the teacher to participate in the construction of the stem. If the supervisor provided the full statement, the teacher would not have to participate in learning how to write that portion of the lesson plan.

The supervisor could also do the opposite and provide a stem with what students would need to *produce*, and allow the teacher to think about the specific *content*. For example, a stem for a language arts lesson about descriptive writing might be this:

> *To begin the lesson I would like you to work with a partner and write down three words that . . .*

The supervisor should not write a full statement, but he/she can modify how much of the stem is provided. Just as teachers differentiate instruction for the needs of their students, a supervisor should differentiate based on the individual needs of each teacher.

Stems in the Closure Section of a Lesson Plan

Similar to the introduction section of a lesson plan, the closure is a brief way to wrap up the lesson by having students quickly participate in an activity that has them reflecting on or applying the content they learned during the lesson. An example of a full closing statement from a geography lesson might be as follows:

> *Reflecting on today's lesson about geographical directions, look at the map of North America and write down what is North, South, East, and West of Colorado.*

Just like the introductory statement, the closing includes a reference to where the statement takes place in the lesson plan, focuses on content, and has an activity for students. However, there are two differences between a closure and introduction.

The first is that the closure statement always connects to the current lesson and is *not* used to launch new content. In this example, the statement informs students that they will be applying content they learned during the lesson. It is important that students apply knowledge, and not be asked to regurgitate information. In this example, the teacher would not have gone over the answer to this particular question during the lesson. Instead, the teacher might have looked at different states or even other countries during the lesson, and then for the closure, the students would be asked to apply their understanding of geographical directions by looking at a different state that they did not discuss during the lesson.

The other key aspect of a closing statement is that it should be a type of formative assessment that directly connects to the lesson's learning objective(s). The closing stem should be reflective of what is written in the learning objectives and assessment portion of the lesson plan.

The second difference is that the activity in the closing statement should be something students either did during the lesson or have done in a previous lesson. The goal of the closure is to assess students' understanding of the content of the lesson, not to assess their ability to complete an activity. For this reason, the activity should be something students would easily be able to do without much direction. The activity should last from one to three minutes.

As in the introductory statement, a supervisor should not provide the full closing statement. The supervisor only provides a stem of the statement. The supervisor should just provide either the procedure or the content portion of the statement. The following is an example of providing the content, and then leaving space for the teacher to think of the activity.

> *Today's lesson in biology focused on genetics. Using your understanding of genetic mapping . . .*

This example demonstrates that the stem is meant for the end of the lesson, and it is a review of specific content covered during the lesson. It leaves space for the teacher to think about the activity. Since novice teachers often struggle with the content and usually are good at developing activities, providing this type of stem helps show the teacher how to include the content but still gives the teacher room to participate in building the stem by playing to the novice teacher's strength of creating an activity. This can build teacher confidence.

Although it is good to play to teachers' strengths and boost their confidence, it is also important to challenge them to think about the content. Providing a closing stem that has the activity is good because it encourages the teacher to think about the content. It also demonstrates how to write a closing stem with a short and simple activity meant to assess the content. Here is an example for a math class:

> *Before you leave class today, spend the last two minutes writing down your work and answers to the following two word problems . . .*

This type of stem helps a teacher understand that it is important to have something at the end of the lesson, gives specific guidelines for how long it should take, and can clearly be connected to the assessment section of a lesson plan. This activity is not glamorous. It does not have bells or whistles. It is direct and something students have probably experienced before.

When providing a closing stem, it is important that the supervisor gets right to the point. This will help the teacher understand the crucial elements.

Stems in the Procedure Section of a Lesson Plan

The procedure section is typically a step-by-step breakdown of what a teacher will be doing during the lesson. Since there is a lot of variety within the procedures about what content is covered and how it is covered, stems in the procedures should get a teacher to think about the content. Novice teachers sometimes get caught up in the fun activity and forget about the content.

When there are procedures that focus on the activity but lack content, the supervisor should write a stem that includes a reference to the fun activity but then pushes the teacher to think about and focus on the content. For example, many novice teachers create lessons that include a debate. The problem is that the lesson plan focuses on the debate and not the content. This is a good time for a supervisor to write a stem. An example of a stem that could be included would be this:

> *Today we will have a debate, but before we do I want to go over the historical significance of... and the key concepts associated with . . .*

When writing a stem to be used in the procedures section, it is important that the supervisor remember that the lesson plan should not only reflect a teacher's understanding of how to create engaging lessons, but demonstrate his/her understanding of the content that needs to be taught. The teacher's writing some of the content within the lesson plan forces the teacher to think about the content prior to instruction and make sure he/she knows the content.

Stems Applicable Throughout the Lesson Plan

Teachers often write lesson plans and focus on the content and activity. Teachers forget that the lesson plan can be a space to think about classroom management. A supervisor can use stems to help a teacher think about classroom management by focusing on directions and behavioral expectations.

The supervisor may use stems to help a teacher think about directions needed for students to complete an activity. For the more novice teacher, or a teacher who struggles with classroom management, the stem should be very specific, giving step-by-step directions. Any activity should be given as a set of two to five directions.

For students in the lower grades, teachers need to realize that developmentally they might only be able to retain two-directional tasks at a time. As students get older, they can retain more information and remember up to five-directional tasks at a time. A stem for directions follows:

> *Before you jump into the activity, I want to go over the directions. You will first . . . . Second you will . . . . Finally you will . . . .*

Once the stem is provided, the teacher can think clearly about those directions. For teachers who are more experienced but need a friendly reminder to go over directions, the supervisor can just give a stem that clearly tells the teacher to think about directions. Here is an example:

> *The directions for today's lesson are . . . .*

In both examples, the stems could be used at any point in the lesson. By thinking through directions ahead of time, teachers can reduce problems in terms of classroom management.

The second method for providing stems throughout the lesson plan is to demonstrate how a teacher might set clear behavioral expectations for how the task will be accomplished.

Classroom teachers often set up an activity, but then get discouraged because of the way students attacked the activity, which was not what the teacher envisioned.

For instance, if a teacher wants students to read a passage and then discuss and answer a series of questions with other students at their table, the lesson plan needs to state clearly how the students are to do the activity. It is not enough to say students should read a passage. It needs to say that the students will read the passage silently. If the teacher wants students to discuss with their group, he/she needs to *write* that students will discuss the passage using inside voices.

These subtle differences will help teachers think about the behavior they want to see from students during the activity. Stems for this method are fill in the blank. The supervisor should write out the direction and leave a space for the teacher to insert modifiers to describe how the students should complete the task(s). For example,

> *Everyone will* ___________ *read the passage, and then in your table group discuss the passage by* ____________________.

This method is helpful for teachers who struggle with classroom management in terms of behavior. It also helps teachers think through an activity and assess why they want students to act in a certain way. Sometimes it is important that students do an activity silently, and sometimes it is important that they are talking and interacting. Teachers need to think about those things and have a good rationale as to why it is important for students to engage in the activity in a specific manner.

Teachers who struggle with classroom management often forget to share their behavioral expectations with the students. If novice teachers do not share with their students how to engage in an activity, the students will decide for themselves, and it might not be what the teacher expected. This type of stem helps teachers think about this as part of their planning and preparation to reduce behavioral problems during class.

The key to using stems is for a supervisor to address a problem, give enough of a stem to support the teacher, but leave it open so the teacher has to do the work of completing the stem. If the supervisor does all the work, the teachers do not learn how to write the statements on their own. They just use whatever the supervisor writes. They will not be challenged to think through it themselves.

It is essential to note that stems should teach the teacher how to think through different aspects of their lessons, which can be transferable to future lessons. Prior to utilizing this method, a supervisor should discuss it with the teacher so the teacher understands what a stem is and that he/she is responsible for completing each statement. Once a teacher receives a lesson plan back with the stems, it is expected that the teacher will take it, review the stems, actually *complete* each stem, and then add them to the lesson plan. This is the only way it will have an impact on their instruction and future planning.

Strategy 2: *Journalistic Approach*

In this approach, the supervisor uses the five Ws—who, what, where, when (and how), and why—to encourage the teacher to think about different aspects of planning a lesson. The following section addresses each of the five Ws as well as two different approaches for how a supervisor can provide written feedback.

The Five Ws

WHO

Who is doing the learning? Often novice teachers are observed doing most of the work in the classroom. When asked, "Who did most of the talking during class?" or "Who did most of the work solving problems and answering questions?" the novice teacher realizes *he/she* did most of the talking and most of the work.

Whoever is doing the work is doing the learning. If that is true, in the lesson plan, a supervisor needs to address "who" is doing the work. For example, a math teacher writes a procedure in his/her lesson plan to go over the math homework:

Review math homework problems.

The supervisor needs to address that the "who" is missing from the procedure. In the margin, the supervisor can write,

Who will be doing the math homework problems?

Sometimes it helps to write what the teacher will be doing, specifically. For example,

I will read the passage aloud and ask questions.

If a teacher constantly writes what he/she will be doing during instruction, and does not clearly state opportunities for students to perform, a supervisor should acknowledge this. Here is an example:

Who is answering the questions?

Although a teacher might think that it is explicit, it is important that they think about specific ways their students are engaging throughout the lesson and make sure the lesson plan is written to include students. A simple question like that can help redirect the teacher.

WHAT

There are two ways of looking for the "what" in a lesson plan. The first is to figure out what students will be doing. In the example of the math homework problems, the supervisor might write,

What homework problems will they review?

This gets a teacher to think about which of the homework problems they should go over. It gives a teacher the chance to think of his/her rationale behind going over specific problems. It also forces the teacher to think about what he/she really wants students to do.

"What" can also be used to ask, What will the *teacher* be doing? Some lesson plans describe students working in groups, completing a task. For example,

Students will work with their table groups to read the chapter and answer the questions at the end of the chapter.

It is great that students are doing the work, but what is the teacher doing during this time? For these situations, the following question can help teachers think about their actions:

What will the teacher be doing during this time?

This forces the teachers to think constantly about what they are doing, and gets them to think about why they are doing it. The purpose of this type of question is to avoid having teachers sit at their desks doing their own work. By doing this, novice teachers can go from simply monitoring students to engaging with small groups or pulling out students who need additional assistance. This strategy helps novice teachers think about differentiation.

WHERE and HOW

"Where" and "how" are grouped together because they are both used to help a teacher think about the directions he/she is giving to students.

- Where will students do the activity?
- How will they complete the activity?
- Where will they show their work?
- Where will they turn in their work?
- How will they act during the activity?

"Where" and "how" helps teachers think about classroom management. For example, a teacher in a science class might write this procedure:

Students will get the materials and begin the lab.

In this situation, the supervisor wants to force the teacher to think about how he/she is setting up the space of the classroom and the behavioral expectations he/she is setting for students. For this example, the supervisor could write the following questions:

Where will students get the materials?
How will they begin the lab? How will they get the materials?

WHEN

"When" is a combination of looking at the learning objectives, assessments, and differentiation sections of the lesson plan, and identifying when those are being attended to in the introduction, procedure, or closing sections of the lesson plan. To do this, the supervisor reads the learning objectives, assessments, and differentiation sections and then goes through the rest of the lesson plan and notes when those are being addressed. For instance, there might be a learning objective that states,

Students will identify the first thirteen states in the United States of America.

When reviewing the lesson plan, the supervisor will want to identify when the teacher is meeting that goal. For example, the teacher might write,

At the front of the class, project an image of a map of the United States from 1788.

This is a good example of "when" the teacher is meeting this learning goal. Of course, this would not be the only time the teacher is meeting this learning goal. "When" questions could be used to challenge a teacher to think of other opportunities to address a learning goal. For example,

When will students fill in their own map of the thirteen states?

"When" questions could also be used if there is a learning objective that is not clearly addressed in the procedures section. I have seen novice teachers include multiple learning objectives, partially because they think they need to, but the lesson does not really address all the objectives. In those situations, the supervisor can ask the teacher to think about when a specific learning objective is being covered.

WHY

"Why" is not as prevalent in teacher lesson plans. Lesson plans often describe the tasks and how those activities will be accomplished. Teachers rarely include the rationale behind the activities. However, novice teachers get caught up in the activity and forget to think about why they are having students engage in different tasks, which sometimes leads the teacher to do more "fun" activities and forget about the learning objectives. For this reason, asking the novice teacher to think about the "why" is important.

"Why" could be asked throughout the lesson plan. For instance, the supervisor can ask why the teacher decided to have students work independently, with partners, or in groups. Teachers should have a rationale. When a teacher writes that students will turn and talk to a partner, the supervisor could write a question such as this:

Why are students doing turn-and-talk rather than talking in a group?

When writing this type of question, the supervisor should ask why they are doing something, and not why aren't they doing something else. The something else is important because the supervisor wants to avoid having the teacher think he/she is doing it "just because." The goal is not to change the teacher's mind, but instead to challenge the teacher to think about whether his/her approach is the best method.

Sometimes the teacher will change what he/she does based on the suggestion given by the supervisor in the "why" question. Other times, the teacher will continue with their original decision, but have a stronger rationale as to why they have decided to do it that way. Either way, the "why" question forces the teacher to think about what he/she wants students to do. That is the backbone behind asking "why?"

Two Approaches for Providing Journalistic Feedback

There are two approaches for providing journalistic feedback. Both approaches use the definitions of the five Ws as described above. In the following subsections, you'll see how to do both approaches.

I. Focused Approach

The *Journalistic Approach* can be done in two different ways. The first way is for the supervisor to focus on one or two of the Ws. Providing comments on lesson plans can be overwhelming for both the supervisor and teacher if there is a lack of focus. Before giving written feedback, the supervisor should advise the teacher to concentrate on one or two Ws. The feedback could be based on something on which the teacher wants to work, or based on previous classroom observations in which a problem was addressed.

The idea behind this approach is to narrow the scope of what a teacher really needs to work on, and not overwhelm the teacher with comments about everything. It also helps a supervisor to read the lesson plan with a focus. Teachers should concentrate on one of the Ws and then pick one after their initial reading of the lesson plan. This helps a teacher decide what he/she wants to work on, and then addresses one other area that might not have been apparent to the teacher that he/she has identified as an area to improve.

For this approach, the supervisor will do an initial reading of the lesson plan. This should be a quick read. Then the supervisor goes through and reads the lesson plan and codes it for one of the five Ws. Each time the supervisor sees the teacher using that W, the supervisor will underline (or highlight) where that W is taking place. By doing this, it acknowledges the use of the W to the teacher. The following is an example of coding a lesson plan that looks at "what" students will do:

> *At table groups, students will work as a group to write down as many different adjectives to describe the flower.*

Identifying when a teacher uses the W is important because sometimes teachers do not know they are doing something until it is pointed out to them. This builds teacher confidence and highlights what they are doing right.

The supervisor reads the lesson plan a third time to identify places where the W should have been used but was missing. The following is an example of a assessment that is missing "who":

> *Write the multi-digit multiplication problem*
> *on the board: 54 × 12 =*

In the margin the supervisor can simply ask a question that identifies the missing "who" from the statement; this forces the teacher to think about who will be doing the work. An example of the question might be this:

> *Who will be solving the math problem?*

The question challenges the teacher to think about who is doing the work of solving the problem. Will the teacher have a student come to the board? Will the teacher have all students solve the problem independently and then have one student demonstrate how he/she did it? Will students work together? Regardless of what a teacher decides to do, the important aspect is that the question forces the teacher to think about it. Pushing teachers to think about the five Ws helps them think through their lessons at a conceptual level.

If the supervisor is coding for just one of the five Ws, he/she will read it a total of three times. If the supervisor is coding for more than one of the five Ws, he/she will have to repeat the second and third round of reading for any additional Ws. This is important because it focuses the supervisor. If a supervisor chooses to do more than one thing per reading, something could easily get missed.

After the lesson has been coded and all comments have been written in the margin, the lesson plan should be returned to the teacher, and the teacher must go back and address each of the questions posed in the margin. This is essential. If the teacher does not do this, then he/she is not learning from the experience by engaging with the feedback.

It must be discussed before using this approach that *the teacher will answer the questions, and integrate them into the lesson plan prior to instruction of the lesson.* This is the only way to get the teacher to reflect on the comments and engage in an activity that changes the way he/she writes a lesson plan.

II. Broad Approach

The second approach is for the supervisor to do a quick coding of the lesson plan for all five Ws and then write in the margin one question for each of them. Let me break this down. The supervisor goes through the lesson plan. Anytime the teacher addresses who, what, where, when (and how) or why, the supervisor underlines it in the lesson plan and then writes which of the five Ws it was in the margin (table 2.1).

Table 2.1. Example of Written Feedback on Lesson Plan

Page Margin	*Lesson Plan*
Who	*The students will work with their partners to complete the science lab.*

Just as in the earlier approach, this builds teacher confidence and shows them what they are doing right. Next, the supervisor reads through the lesson plan and picks five places to write a question using each of the five Ws. By doing one of each of the five Ws, it helps the teacher think about all five, but by limiting it to one question for each, it does not overwhelm the teacher.

Ultimately, the lesson plan is given back to the teacher. The teacher must address each of the five questions in the margin and insert changes into the lesson plan addressing each of those questions. Then the teacher must answer each of the following five questions:

1. Based on the coding, which of the five Ws did you use the most?
2. Based on the coding, which of the five Ws did you use the least?
3. Describe two patterns you noticed about how or when you used the Ws.
4. Looking at the data from questions 1–3, what specific changes are you going to make to this lesson plan? (*This is in addition to addressing the questions in the margin.*)
5. Describe one thing you will take away from this feedback and apply to your next lesson plan.

These five questions force the teacher to look closely at the coding and reflect on it in a meaningful way.

Both approaches require multiple readings from the supervisor and force a teacher to reflect on the written feedback and make changes to the lesson plan prior to instruction. These approaches will also help a teacher think about key elements of instruction that can be transferable to future lesson plans. The goal is to provide written feedback about the five Ws in a way that a teacher can use in the future, not just for one individual lesson plan.

WRITTEN FEEDBACK BENEFITS, DRAWBACKS, AND TIPS

There are two main benefits associated with written feedback. The first is that it provides feedback prior to instruction. It forces a teacher to revisit the lesson before actually teaching it. This means a teacher would have thought through the lesson during the initial writing of the lesson plan, and then again after receiving the written feedback. The more opportunities a teacher has to think through content and his/her instructional practices prior to teaching, the greater potential the lesson has to be a stronger lesson.

The other benefit is that it does not require the supervisor giving feedback to observe the actual lesson or meet with the teacher. Due to time constraints, it might be difficult for the principal, colleague, or supervisor to observe the lesson or find time to have a meeting. However, the teacher or prospective teacher can still be given support and be challenged to think about the content and pedagogy through the written feedback.

A drawback is the timeliness. For written feedback to be effective, the teacher must provide the written lesson plan ahead of time, and the supervisor must be able to read the lesson and provide the written feedback in a timely fashion so that the teacher has a chance to review the feedback and make corrections to the lesson plan prior to teaching. This means the turn-around time must be quick.

Lesson plans are not often written more than a week in advance. There needs to be a commitment from the supervisor and teacher about when it will take place and how long each person has to work on it. If the written feedback is not given back to the teacher with enough time for the teacher to reflect on it and make the changes, then the impact of the written feedback is not going to have the maximum benefit.

For optimal benefit, supervisors and teachers should negotiate a realistic number of lesson plans for written feedback, and agree on a timeline. The goal is not to provide written feedback for every lesson. The idea is to provide it for one lesson plan, and then have a teacher use that written feedback for that lesson and apply it to future lesson plans.

Written feedback can be given to a teacher across multiple lesson plans, though it should also be spaced out over a period of time to see the growth. For the most novice teacher, providing written feedback on one lesson per week works. With more experienced teachers, the written feedback can be spaced out. Again, this will vary depending on the relationship of the supervisor and teacher, and depending where on the spectrum the teacher lies in terms of needing support. Regardless, it needs to be discussed and agreed upon by both parties.

The other suggestion is that the supervisor and teacher agree upon a strategy. It is not suggested to use both strategies simultaneously or to go back and forth between the two strategies. It is important that both parties agree upon which strategy they are using and then use that strategy for at least five lessons. That gives a teacher the chance to really improve his/her lessons, and apply the comments from written feedback on a lesson plan to future lesson plans. If there is not consistency with the type of feedback, a teacher and supervisor will not see the long-term effects of either strategy.

Providing written feedback should not take the place of observing a teacher. This allows continual support for a teacher outside of the classroom, but it should not replace having a supervisor see how a lesson plan is executed in real time.

As long as these suggestions are kept in mind when providing written feedback, teachers will improve their content and instruction prior to implementing a lesson and consider different elements when planning and preparing for instruction.

3

PROVIDING ORAL FEEDBACK ON LESSON PLANS

Student teachers, novice teachers, and experienced teachers being evaluated are all required to write lesson plans. For those lesson plans, they need constructive feedback. Chapter 2 discussed ways to provide written feedback before instruction, but supervisors also need strategies for providing oral feedback. Unlike written feedback, which is provided pre-instruction, oral feedback can take place before *or* after instruction. There are different rationales for providing it before versus after instruction, and different methods for doing it based on when the feedback is given. In this chapter, you will learn the rationale, methods, benefits, drawbacks, and tips for providing oral feedback on lesson plans before and after instruction.

Strategy 3: *Lesson Plan Walk Through*

Rationale

Providing oral feedback before instruction is designed for a teacher to think through a specific lesson with the intention of making systematic changes to the content, pedagogical practices, and/or the classroom management techniques for that given lesson. This strategy is called the *Lesson Plan Walk Through*. The teacher provides a written copy of the lesson plan to his/her supervisor and then meets to walk through the lesson plan orally before instruction. By walking through the lesson, the teacher has an opportunity to think through the content and different practices he/she has thought about using for that particular lesson, and be challenged to think about different components of the lesson. As the teacher walks through the lesson, the supervisor asks a series of both planned and impromptu questions. Questions are not designed to be judgmental. They are designed to push a teacher to think critically about the lesson and make changes based on a critical reflection.

The objective of the *Lesson Plan Walk Through* is for teachers to have a rationale behind what they are teaching, how they are teaching it, and why they have decided to teach it that way. Although the *Lesson Plan Walk Through* is for one specific lesson, the process will be an educative tool that teachers can use as they plan for future lessons.

Methods

There are multiple steps to the *Lesson Plan Walk Through*, and specific responsibilities of the teacher and supervisor for this process to be a positive experience. To begin, the teacher must write the lesson plan before meeting with his/her supervisor. The lesson that is selected must be a lesson a teacher has not taught, but has planned and wants to improve.

It might be a lesson in which the content is difficult or new to a teacher. For example, a teacher who has never taught a science lesson about condensation might want to engage in a *Lesson Plan Walk Through* to ensure the content is correct and the practices match the content. It could also be a lesson in which a teacher wants to try a different methodology and he/she wants help thinking through the lesson before executing a new teaching practice. For example, a teacher who has never implemented centers might want to use this method of feedback before implementing centers for the first time.

The goal of the teacher should be to get help and feedback on a particular lesson that he/she has some trepidation about, either content, pedagogical, or classroom management. The teacher must approach the experience as a time to reflect on the lesson, make necessary changes to the written lesson, and not be defensive when being asked questions about his/her lesson or rationale for why he/she did or did not include certain information. To reduce the risk of a teacher becoming defensive about the feedback or process involved in this feedback, it is helpful for the teacher to select the lesson.

The *Lesson Plan Walk Through* needs to happen at least a day before the lesson will be implemented so that the teacher has sufficient time to make any modifications, and prepare for those modifications (i.e., getting supplies/materials). For instance, a teacher might make content changes to a worksheet. A teacher might also decide to alter his/her centers. For these reasons, the *Lesson Plan Walk Through* must take place at least one day prior.

The supervisor must have adequate time to read the lesson and design a series of questions. These must be reflective questions about information that is evident in the lesson plans, or information the supervisor thinks is missing from the written lesson plan. The questions fall into three categories: (1) pedagogy, (2) content, or (3) classroom management.

Lesson Plan Walk Through: *Pedagogy*

The first category of questions focuses on challenging a teacher's pedagogical practices. Table 3.1 is an example from a lesson plan about adding fractions. The example comes from the closure (wrap-up) section of a lesson plan.

In response to the written lesson plan, the supervisor would need to prepare a set of questions that were directed at the pedagogy, challenging a teacher to make a change, and then encouraging the teacher to provide a rationale behind their decision.

Table 3.1. Example of Supervisor's Prepared Pedagogical Questions for Oral Feedback

Example of Lesson Plan Closure	*Example of Supervisor's Prepared Questions*
Tell students that today they learned how to add fractions, and tonight's homework would reinforce that skill.	Is there an action verb you could use to replace "tell"? If so, what is the word? Why did you select that word? If need be, what other changes to the wrap-up would you make to accommodate that new word selection? Why make those changes?

In this example, the pedagogical goal is to move a teacher away from "telling" students, and instead pushing a teacher to use language that has students doing the work and doing the learning, as opposed to the teaching doing the work. Keep in mind that the supervisor is not spoon-feeding the teacher and giving the word replacement. That must come from the teacher.

The supervisor is asking direct questions from which a teacher can begin to think about his/her pedagogical practices and make changes to the lesson that work for the teacher. The supervisor cannot give the ideas, and the supervisor needs to be okay with whatever the teacher decides as long as the teacher has a rationale for it. It might not be the exact idea of the supervisor, but the goal is not to create clones of the supervisor. The goal is for the supervisor to guide the teacher through a line of questioning so that the teacher can derive his/her own ideas based on pedagogical practices. By having the teacher come up with his/her own ideas, there is more likelihood that the teacher will implement them when giving the lesson, and hopefully think about those pedagogical goals when constructing and implementing future lessons.

Lesson Plan Walk Through: *Content*

The second category of questions focuses on the content of a lesson plan. In a lesson plan, the teacher typically focuses on pedagogy and classroom management and usually provides very brief information about the content. The questions a supervisor prepares before the *Lesson Plan Walk Through* will focus on getting a teacher to think through the content by developing definitions, creating examples, and predicting misconceptions or questions students might have. The supervisor will use these three categories to develop content questions in preparation for the *Lesson Plan Walk Through*.

Table 3.2 is an excerpt of the introduction and beginning section of the procedures of a lesson plan about the White House. In the column marked "Supervisor's Prepared Questions," the questions have been coded into three categories: Definitions (D), Examples (E), or Students Questions/Misconceptions (S).

These questions are not meant to challenge a teacher's content knowledge. They are designed to ask teachers questions to deepen their understanding of the content. A supervisor must think about how and when a teacher will answer these content questions. If a supervisor asks questions and demands that a teacher answer these questions on the spot, it could discourage the teacher and make the teacher feel uncomfortable. This can cause him/her to become defensive or closed

Table 3.2. Example of Supervisor's Prepared Content Questions for Oral Feedback

Introduction and Beginning Procedures for White House Lesson Plan	*Supervisor's Prepared Content Questions*
Introduction When students walk into the class, there would be five pictures of United States presidents (Washington, Adams, Lincoln, Kennedy, and Obama). Students at table groups would be asked to identify each president and place in chronological order of when they served as president.	Who is in each picture? What years did they serve? [D]
Procedures 1. Go over the introduction activity. 2. Ask students, who from the list was the only president not to live in the White House? This is a good transition into the White House. The White House is located in Washington, D.C. 3. Adams was the first president to live in the White House, but it was constructed while Washington was in office. Give a little background information about the construction of the White House and show pictures. *[Lesson Plan Would Continue]*	What are two important facts about each president? [E][S] Who didn't live in the White House, and why didn't he live there? [D] Where is Washington, D.C., and why is the nation's capital located there? [D] Can you locate Washington D.C. on a map? [E] What does D.C. stand for? [S] Who constructed the White House, and when was it built? [D]

off to the experience. Instead, a supervisor needs to pose the questions as a learning opportunity. Before asking the questions, the supervisor should let the teacher know that he/she is confident in the teacher's content knowledge, and these questions are not a quiz to test his/her understanding of the content. The more the supervisor can reduce a teacher's anxiety, the better.

There are three approaches for having teachers answer content questions. The first is to allow a teacher to answer any questions he/she wants to on the spot. For instance, the question asking a teacher what *D.C.* stands for might be something the teacher knows offhand and can quickly answer. There will be these types of content questions that the teacher knows and just wants to check off. These questions can sometimes build a teacher's confidence because they can demonstrate his/her knowledge.

The second approach is to give a teacher time. A supervisor can pose the questions, and a teacher can listen to the questions and choose which questions to come back to later in the conference. For example, the question asking the teacher for two facts about each president might be something the teacher can just go back to on his/her own. These might not be content questions that are essential for the teacher to answer during the conference because it is not imperative content for the particular lesson. It is content that will just enhance the teacher's overall understanding of the topic. Allowing a teacher to work on questions after the conference shows that the supervisor trusts the teacher to continue his/her learning on his/her own.

The third approach is to have the teacher and supervisor work together to answer the questions. For example, the question asking about who constructed the White House and when it was built is very specific and is essential to the lesson. The teacher might know the information, but if not, it is good to research it together, and from that research the teacher and supervisor might find other interesting pieces of information. The additional content that is discovered during that time might add to the teacher's lesson or impact what he/she decides to share during instruction. Working together on these questions shows the teacher that the supervisor is also willing to learn the content and that the supervisor does not know everything.

All three approaches can and should be used throughout a *Lesson Plan Walk Through*. The supervisor must read the lesson plan and write these questions ahead of time. The supervisor does not need to look up the answers. The questions are not meant to be a quiz. Instead, the supervisor should plan these questions, but through interaction between the teacher and supervisor allow the conference to be organic. The supervisor might come into the conference with some ideas about how to approach the questions, which is okay, but the supervisor must also allow the teacher to make some decisions about what he/she wants to answer on the spot, what to take home, and what to research with the supervisor.

Lesson Plan Walk Through: *Classroom Management*

The final component of the *Lesson Plan Walk Through* examines the classroom management identified or missing in a lesson plan. Classroom management can oftentimes be the most challenging aspect of a novice teacher's instructional practice. This is because novice teachers are taught techniques (e.g., turn off the lights to get students quiet) or how to observe for good practices (e.g., watch how experienced teachers get students' attention), but are not taught how to plan intentionally for classroom management.

What does it mean to plan classroom management intentionally? This means the teacher needs to think what students will complete in each task of a lesson and when and how students will complete each task of a lesson. While reviewing a written lesson plan, the supervisor will continually ask four questions:

1. Who is doing the activity/task? *Identify what the students, teacher, volunteer are doing.*
2. What are students doing? *Detailed description of the task step-by-step.*
3. When will students do it? *The time it will take to do the task.*
4. How will students complete the task? *A description of the observable behaviors a teacher expects to see from students.*

These questions will be asked throughout the lesson for each new task or activity presented in the lesson plan. A teacher typically has a variety of activities in a lesson. First comes a warm-up or introductory activity to get students engaged. During the main procedure section of a lesson, a teacher might have two or three activities (e.g., read aloud, mini-lesson, group activity, student presentations, etc.). Finally, a teacher might have a closure or wrap-up for students to do before dismissing the class or moving to the next lesson. Textbox 3.1 is an abbreviated, written lesson plan of a language arts lesson about sequencing. The information is limited, and there is little to no content or pedagogy provided.

For each new task/activity, the supervisor would ask a series of questions to determine if the teacher has thought about who, what, when, and how the activities are being completed. If the teacher has addressed one or more of these questions in the written lesson plan, the supervisor does not need to ask the teacher to repeat, but it is good for the supervisor to note that the teacher has identified each component. In the example (table 3.3), each activity from the lesson plan is broken down.

Textbox 3.1. Language Arts Lesson Plan about Sequencing

Introduction

When students walk into their English class, have them free read.

Procedures

1. Class read aloud.
2. Complete worksheet about the sequencing of the read aloud book.
3. Go over the worksheet.
4. Each table group will have an envelope with a series of pictures of a child's day. Put them in order.

Closure

Before students leave, ask, "What are some ways to help you remember or identify the sequence of a story?"

For each one there is a series of classroom management questions the supervisor would plan ahead of time to ask the teacher during the *Lesson Plan Walk Through*.

The questions should be prepared before the *Lesson Plan Walk Through* simply by having the supervisor read the lesson and make note of each new activity and whether or not the teacher has identified the who, what, when, and how. During the supervisor and teacher discussion, the supervisor should pose the questions to the teacher. The teacher can immediately answer the questions, or the teacher and supervisor can have a discussion about what might be best. For each activity, the teacher and supervisor will want to write something that addresses each component. Table 3.4 is an example of how the supervisor and teacher could work together to construct the introductory activity for the sequencing lesson that addresses who, what, when, and how.

For an experienced teacher, this level of detail for thinking through a lesson plan and the classroom management might seem extreme, but that is because an experienced teacher might think about those components automatically. A novice teacher might not think about that level of

Table 3.3. Language Arts Lesson Plan about Sequencing with Supervisor's Prepared Content Questions for Oral Feedback

Written Lesson Plan	*Supervisor's Prepared Classroom Management Questions*
Introduction Activity/Task	
When students walk into their English class, have them free read.	***Who?*** What will the teacher be doing during this time? ***What*** will students free read? Do they already have this book, and where is it located? If they don't have a book, where could they get one? Do they know this? ***When?*** How long will they have to free read? ***How?*** Do you want this to be independent? Do you want it silent? *Note: In this example the "who" has been addressed in the teacher's lesson plan as the student, but the lesson plan is missing what the teacher will be doing during that time.*
Procedures Activities/Tasks	
1. Class read aloud.	***Who*** will be reading the book? Who will be listening? ***What*** book will you read for the read aloud? ***When*** or how long do you anticipate the read aloud? ***How*** do you want students to behave during the read aloud?
2. Complete worksheet about the sequencing of the read aloud book.	***Who*** will do the worksheet? What will the teacher do during this time? ***When*** or how long will students have to complete the worksheet? ***How*** will they complete it? In groups? Independently? Silently? Quietly? *Note: In this example the "what" has been addressed in the teacher's lesson plan, so the supervisor does not need to include it.*

(continued)

Table 3.3. *(Continued)*

Written Lesson Plan	*Supervisor's Prepared Classroom Management Questions*
3. Go over the worksheet.	***Who*** will go over it and lead that conversation? ***What*** specifically will they be going over in terms of the worksheet? ***When*** or how long will students have to complete this task? ***How*** will students do this? Is this a whole class activity? Or is this a group or partner activity? If class, will the teacher do the talking and students listen, or will students be called on to share parts of their worksheet while other students listen?
4. Each table group will have an envelope with a series of pictures of a child's day. As a table group, work collaboratively, and quietly to put them in order.	***Who?*** What students will be doing is covered, but what will the teacher do during this time? ***When*** or how long will table groups have to do this? *Note: In this example the "what" and "how" have been addressed in the teacher's lesson plan.*
Closure Activity/Task	
For the last two minutes of class, the teacher will ask: What are some ways students can remember or identify the sequence of a story?	***How*** will students respond? Will students do this as a think-pair-share? Or will you pose the question and have students raise their hands and then call on 3–5 students to share? *Note: In this example, the "who," "what," and "when" have been addressed in the teacher's lesson plan.*

Table 3.4. Supervisor's and Teacher's Revisions of a Lesson Plan

Original Written Lesson Plan	*Revised Written Lesson Plan Addressing Who, What, When, and How*
Introduction Activity/Task When students walk into their English class, have them free read.	**Revised Introduction Activity/Task** As students walk into class, there will be a note posted on the chalkboard directing students to get their own free reading book from their desk or classroom library, and that they have 10 minutes of silent free read. The teacher will model the desired behavior by reading his/her own book.

detail when planning for instruction. By asking these questions during a *Lesson Plan Walk Through*, the supervisor challenges a teacher to think about these things. When asking these questions, the supervisor should not assume that the teacher has not thought about these components; however, the teacher might not have thought about these items in terms of lesson planning.

During the *Lesson Plan Walk Through,* the supervisor must make clear that the teacher needs to consider these items, but the supervisor needs to recognize that they might change during instruction. A teacher might think about each task and the amount of time it will take; however, during instruction the teacher might assess the students' progress and decide to give students additional time on a particular activity. That is okay because the teacher has thought about every aspect of the lesson and will know how to reshape the lesson to accommodate those changes.

If the teacher hasn't thought through all the tasks and how each task will be implemented, he/she might not be as successful in practice when needing to reshape the lesson. Thinking through the classroom management will give novice teachers confidence in how each activity and task will be completed and how the overall lesson will run. The confidence will also allow a novice teacher to be flexible during instruction. As a novice teacher gains experience, these classroom management items in a lesson plan will become more automatic and less evident.

Strategy 4: *Compare and Contrast*

Rationale

Providing post-instruction feedback always focuses on what happened during instructional time. It does not focus on the written lesson plans. Feedback on written lesson plans is typically given before instruction so that modifications can be made to the written lesson plan before instruction. That type of feedback has direct implications on that specific lesson.

This feedback is unique because it is the only oral feedback given to teachers after instruction that focuses on the written lesson plans. The aim of this unique type of feedback is to challenge a teacher to think about what happened during instruction (good and bad) and compare that to what he/she wrote for the lesson plan. This experience pushes teachers to identify the aspects of their instruction that might not be present when they plan for instruction. The goal is not to change instructional practices, but to shape teachers' planning for instruction to make them more intentional in how they plan, so that the plan aligns with the type of instructional practices they want to employ.

Methods

Providing oral feedback post-instruction is designed to have teachers reflect on their instruction in relation to how they planned for that specific lesson, and use it to transform how they plan for future lessons. This will help make teachers' lesson plans more aligned with how they instruct. This will also help teachers focus during the planning stages and think through essential aspects of their instruction.

Oral feedback post-instruction is the only feedback described in this book that requires that the supervisor watch the entire lesson. For the other types of feedback, a supervisor might choose to watch how the lesson is executed, but this is the only feedback that actually uses what happens during instruction as part of the feedback process. It is beneficial to watch in person; however, there might be situations that prevent a supervisor from being physically present during the time of instruction. For example, there are more opportunities for student teachers to do their student teaching abroad. For those types of circumstances, a supervisor can either have the lesson videotaped, or, if technology is available, the supervisor can video conference the lesson so they are watching in real time.

There are three sequential parts to the *Compare and Contrast* method. The first is the initial read through of the lesson plan. This is quick, and takes place a day before instruction. Next, is the observation.

As mentioned earlier, this is the only lesson plan feedback that does require the supervisor to watch the execution of the lesson in its entirety. Finally, there is the debrief conference.

Compare and Contrast: *Initial Read Through*

The supervisor is given the written lesson plan before instruction so that he/she can read through it one time and be prepared to take good notes during instruction. When the supervisor reads through the lesson plan for structure, he/she is looking for specific components. Based on an assortment of lesson plan models, the following is a checklist of components a supervisor would want to look for when doing the quick read:

- Standards
- Learning Objectives
- Introduction/Warm-up Activity
- Procedures
- Closure/Wrap-up Activity
- Formative Assessment (if applicable, summative)
- Differentiation
- Materials

This is not a comprehensive list, and a university, school, or district might have a predesigned lesson plan outline or components that are required for their lesson plans. Whether it is this list, a predesigned lesson plan outline, or something the supervisor has constructed, the supervisor wants to have some form of checklist for components that should be present in the lesson plan. This will allow the supervisor to do the quick initial read through and note that the essential components are present (or missing). If any components are missing, the supervisor should make a note of them and include it in the debriefing conference. This should not be discussed before the instruction of the lesson.

The second aspect of the read through is for a supervisor to get a general understanding of the content being taught and how it will be taught. For instance, if it is a science lesson, the supervisor might read a written lesson plan and learn that the class will be learning about the pH scale and doing a lab exercise to test different liquid solutions for their pH balance. Or, a supervisor might review a lesson that is about the

Civil War, and during class students will be doing research and holding a debate between the South and North. Both lessons have very different content and different pedagogical styles.

Reading the lesson plan before instruction will give a supervisor the opportunity to prepare for what he/she will be observing. The more prepared the supervisor is for what he/she will observe, the better notes the supervisor can take during instruction. Again, the goal is not for the supervisor to determine if the content and/or pedagogy is what the supervisor would choose to do during instruction. The initial read through is to prepare the supervisor for what he/she will observe during instruction so he/she can be prepared and know what to watch for.

Since the initial read through is to provide the supervisor with a general overview of what he/she will observe during class time so that the supervisor can take good notes during instruction, it is imperative that the supervisor not make comments on the lesson plan before instruction. The goal of this approach is to compare the lesson plan to instruction. If notes are taken beforehand, then the feedback is not solely based on the comparison between the plan and instruction. For this reason, lesson plans should be given twenty-four hours before instruction. This is enough time for the supervisor to prepare, but not too much time that would result in giving feedback on the written lesson plan. However, this can be negotiated between the supervisor and teacher ahead of time.

Compare and Contrast: *Observation*

During the observation, the supervisor will take extensive notes. For this reason the supervisor should practice this method multiple times before using it in a post-oral-feedback session. Supervisors might also find it helpful to receive the written lesson plan electronically so that they can take notes on the computer during instruction.

Notes fall under two categories. The first is a running record of everything the supervisor observes during that period of the lesson plan. Whether it was in the written lesson plan or not, the supervisor just keeps a running record of everything that happens during instruction. If possible, the supervisor includes time periods of when events take place. The running record should be objective, without bias (if possible). Textbox 3.2 is an example of a running record for the introduction/warm-up activity of a math lesson.

Textbox 3.2. Example of a Running Record

Introduction Activity/Task

1:00 Teacher (T) has warm-up posted on the whiteboard. Students (S) are coming in, handing in homework in the "homework" bin near T's desk and sitting at their own desk. Reading the whiteboard and beginning to work independently.

1:02 T goes around to Ss (about 5) checking their work on the warm-up problem. Gives some Ss some assistance.

1:05 Some Ss finish. They seem to be helping or talking to other Ss at their table.

1:07 T claps hands, Ss do a responsive clap. This goes back and forth three times. Class is quiet, teacher begins. T cold calls on one S to come to board to solve math problem. This was an S whom the T went to and checked in with during the warm-up.

The running record keeps track of what is happening during that part of the lesson but is void of specifics. Those supplemental details are used during the *Compare and Contrast* conference to provide a more robust picture of the lesson. Supplemental details include quotes, teacher and student examples, questions being asked and answered, pictures of the classroom, and so on. The example in table 3.5 is an extension of the running record from textbox 3.2, made by adding supplemental details.

The supplemental details are taken simultaneously to the running record, which is why these details cannot include everything. There is bias as to what the supervisor chooses to include. That is why the initial read through of the lesson plan before instruction (for the supervisor to identify the content that will be taught, pedagogy, and sequence of events) is important. Although instruction may vary from the written lesson plan, the read through gives some context and allows the supervisor to be somewhat intentional as to what to listen for or look for in terms of the supplemental details.

One approach a supervisor could use for the supplemental details is to look for missing pieces of the written lesson plan. For example,

Table 3.5. Example of Running Record with Supervisor's Supplemental Details

Running Record	*Supplemental Details*
Introduction Activity/Task	
1:00 Teacher (T) has warm-up posted on the whiteboard. Students (S) are coming in, handing in homework in the "homework" bin near T's desk and sitting at their own desk. Reading the whiteboard and beginning to work independently.	On the board: $7 + 3 \times \frac{1}{2} - \frac{3}{4} \times 5 =$
1:02 T goes around to Ss checking their on the warm-up problem. Gives some Ss some assistance.	Four of the students helped were at front table group near teacher desk. The other student was a boy who sat near back door. Did not get to three of the five table groups.
1:05 Some Ss finish. They seem to be helping or talking to other Ss at their table.	
1:07 T claps hands, Ss do a responsive clap. This goes back and forth three times. Class is quiet, teacher begins. T cold calls on one S to come to board to solve math problem. This was an S whom the T went to and checked in with during the warm-up.	"This problem is not just about fractions, I hope you all remembered the order of operations."

student teachers and novice teachers may struggle with classroom management. The supervisor might read the written lesson plan and notice a dearth of classroom management details (i.e., giving instructions, identifying times for tasks, etc.), and use that as the focus for collecting supplemental details. Table 3.6 is a small portion of a lesson plan that examines the introductory activity, and the first part of the mini-lesson. The example includes the running record and the supplemental details, with specific focus given to classroom management. The supervisor recorded evidence of providing (or not providing) instructions to students to complete different tasks, time limits for activities, directions for whom students should work with, and expectations for how students should accomplish each task.

The example (table 3.6) highlights the running record and the supplemental details that a supervisor would make during the course of the observation. Although the supplemental details are biased in terms of what the supervisor chose to include, the actual running record and supple-

Table 3.6. Example of Running Record with Supervisor's Supplemental Details and Focus on Classroom Management

Lesson Plan	*Running Record*	*Supplemental Details*
Introduction Activity/Task Students come in for a silent read of a book of their choice for first five minutes. **Mini-Lesson** "Today we are going to talk about setting." Ask students to describe the setting from their silent reading book. *[Lesson Plan Would Continue]*	**12:00** On the board: Come in and silent read. Teacher is reading her own book. Some students are whispering to each other.	***Teacher:*** "Shhhh. We only have a little longer."
	12:10 Begins lesson by asking students to describe the setting. Calls on three students to share.	
	12:20 Asks students to turn and talk to share their settings. Walks around listening to students.	***Teacher:*** "Its great all of you want to share, but this is taking a little long. Let's turn, talk, and then share. Start, and once I notice everyone has shared, we will come back as a class." ***Student:*** "Who do I share with?" ***Teacher:*** "Anyone at your table group."
	12:30 Calls on three more students to share.	***Teacher:*** "Not everyone can share today so I'll use the popsicle jar with names to pick randomly so it is fair."

mental details are written without bias. It is what the supervisor hears and sees. This will allow for a conversation to take place about what happened during instruction compared to how the teacher planned for instruction, rather than a conversation about what the supervisor believes should happen during instruction.

Compare and Contrast: *Debrief*

After the lesson takes place, the teacher and supervisor find time to meet and debrief. This time should be negotiated between the two parties. Some teachers will ask to not meet immediately following the lesson. Teachers might need time to step away from the lesson and just reflect on the instruction themselves. Removing themselves from the lesson for a few hours or even a day will allow the teacher to reflect and not feel defensive about his/her instruction. However, the debrief should not take place more than one day after the lesson because the teacher and supervisor will have forgotten some aspects, and the lesson will not feel as fresh. Some teachers might choose to meet immediately after the lesson. Debrief sessions last at least one hour.

To begin the debrief, a copy of the initial written lesson plan should be given to the teacher, without any of the supervisor's notes. The teacher should skim his/her own lesson plan and make three simple notations next to each component, task, or activity of the lesson plan (see table 3.7).

The teacher should only spend two to three minutes doing this. This should be quick. It is just a way for the teacher to quickly remember his/her written lesson and reflect on his/her instruction.

The teacher should then be given the supervisor's running record (not the supplemental details). The teacher is given time to read through the running record along with the written lesson plan. With a different color pen, the teacher is asked to make the same notations on the written lesson plan based on the running record.

After the notations are made, the supervisor uses a series of questions to lead the debrief conversation (see table 3.8). The supervisor

Table 3.7. Notations for the *Compare and Contrast* Debrief

	Notation
Component, task, or activity that the teacher believes he/she did not do during instruction.	–
Component, task, or activity that the teacher believes he/she did during the lesson, and aligns closely to what he/she wrote in the lesson plan.	+
Component, task, or activity the teacher believes he/she did during the lesson but adapted or modified during instruction, so it might not directly align.	o

Table 3.8. Debrief Questions for the Running Record

Questions for "+"	*Questions for "o"*	*Questions for "–"*
What components of your written lesson plan were aligned "+" with your instruction based on the running record? Why do you think those components closely aligned? Based on your initial reflection notations, did you identify those elements as being aligned to your instruction? Why or why not?	What components of your written lesson plan were adapted/modified "o" based on the running record? Why do you think those elements were adapted/modified? What was happening during instruction? Based on your initial reflection notations, did you identify those elements as being adapted/modified to your instruction? Why or why not? Knowing how you adapted/modified those elements, what could you do differently when planning a future lesson? Make one change to a lesson for tomorrow that applies.	What components of your written lesson plan were not present in the running record "–"? Do you think those elements of the lesson plan should have been in your instruction? Why or why not? If so, how would you plan differently to make sure those elements come through during instruction? If not, which elements could you take out of your lesson planning to reduce the work?

should ask each set of questions and allow the teacher to reflect. These questions also require a teacher to think about how to apply this new information to future lesson planning. This is a conversation, and a supervisor should feel comfortable engaging in ideas and helping a teacher think through how his/her practice will change.

In addition to these questions, the supervisor may ask if there was an element or component of the lesson plan that was missing, based on a predesigned lesson plan outline. If an element was missing, the supervisor may ask why the teacher did not include it. This could lead to a conversation about whether or not the element was necessary for the teacher.

The second part of the debrief focuses on the supplemental details. The supplemental details focus on an aspect of the teacher's instruction and highlight specific elements of instruction (i.e., classroom management, teacher questions, time management, etc.). The supplemental details should be given to the teacher to read through. Once the teacher has read the details, the supervisor should ask what the teacher thinks. The question should be left open and space given to the teacher to reflect on what it really means to him/her.

After the teacher has reflected, the supervisor can identify specific details to describe patterns he/she notices. For example, the teacher might identify three content questions the teacher asked during the lesson. From that, the supervisor might ask the teacher to reflect on the type of content questions being asked, and ask the teacher to think about some higher order questions that could have been asked. That could lead to a conversation about writing one or two higher order questions for future lesson plans.

Another example would be if the supervisor identified the number of times the teacher had to stop and pause the lesson to review instructions for each activity. That could then lead to a conversation about writing out directions for each activity in the lesson plan so that the teacher would remember during instruction to state directions clearly before a task begins.

The point of this part of the debrief is for the supervisor to use the supplemental details to identify one or at most two patterns that the teacher could then use to inform his/her future lesson planning.

The final aspect of the debrief is for the teacher and supervisor to write clearly two to three practices the teacher will directly apply to writing lesson plans. For example, the teacher "will include two higher order thinking questions in the written lesson plan to ask students during instruction." Or, the teacher "will include times for each activity in his/her lesson plan."

Some of the practices might be to reduce information that is included in the written lesson plans. Oftentimes, novice teachers will include teacher talk. Based on the debrief, the teacher and supervisor might write a goal for the teacher to eliminate teacher talk in the lesson plan.

Although many practices will be discussed during the debrief, setting goals of two to three practices allows the teacher to make small immediate changes to his/her lesson planning practice that will hopefully impact instruction. This makes it manageable, and realistic, for teachers.

The supervisor should follow up with the teacher about a week after the debrief to ask how the two to three practices have been implemented in the writing of other lesson plans. This is not a way to police the teacher; it is just a way to show support.

ORAL FEEDBACK BENEFITS, DRAWBACKS, AND TIPS

Meetings between teachers and supervisors tend to be general, about a teacher's overall performance review (in and outside the classroom) and oftentimes superficial. Supervisors tell what they saw, what they believe needs to be changed, and what future steps they expect to take place. Sometimes, teachers are asked their feelings about their teaching, or are asked to set their own goals based on the supervisor's recommendation. The two methods of oral feedback proposed in this chapter change the discussion from general (or superficial) to a focus on a specific aspect of a teacher's practice. The results from both oral feedback methods move past discussing how a teacher might feel about how he/she plans lessons and how he/she feels about their instruction, and instead challenge teachers to think about what works (and does not work) in terms of planning for instruction.

Another major benefit of providing oral feedback is that it creates a professional space for a teacher and supervisor to work collaboratively. There are limited opportunities for student teachers and novice teachers to get to know supervisors and demonstrate their professionalism; having oral feedback sessions creates these authentic interactions.

One of the goals for both types of oral feedback is that the lesson plan is used as an educative tool, and the conversations lead to changes in how a teacher plans for instruction. However, one of the additional benefits of the *Lesson Plan Walk Through* is that the discussion can have positive implications for the actual lesson that has been discussed. One of the drawbacks to the *Compare and Contrast* is that when the discussion takes place, the lesson has already been taught. So results for that conversation will only have implications for future lesson planning.

Another drawback of oral feedback is that both the supervisor and teacher much carve out time to meet. For the *Compare and Contrast*, the debrief needs to take place within a day, and for the *Lesson Plan Walk Through*, the conversation must happen at least a day before instruction. The *Lesson Plan Walk Through* is also a challenge because the teacher must write the lesson early enough to provide it to the supervisor to read and comment on before meeting. Preparing ahead of time can be difficult for the teacher, and reserving the time to review the lesson plan before meeting can be laborious for supervisors. Finding time for both approaches is challenging but crucial for the success of either type of oral feedback.

In addition to these drawbacks, there is always the risk that either the teacher or supervisor does not feel comfortable. The teacher feels he/she is being evaluated, and as a result, the teacher might not be honest about his/her practices. This can lead to one (or both) parties becoming defensive and not taking full advantage of developing a collaborative, professional relationship. It also paralyzes a teacher's ability to make effective changes to his/her lesson planning practices in a way that will benefit instruction and future lesson planning habits.

To reduce the risk of these drawbacks, there are three tips every supervisor should do before engaging in the *Lesson Plan Walk Through* or *Compare and Contrast* feedback strategies.

The first is for the supervisor to explain clearly the approach that will be used, why the supervisor chose that approach, and the goal(s) of the approach. The supervisor can provide part of this chapter to the teacher to read beforehand so that he/she is aware of the approach. However, the supervisor should not just assign reading. The supervisor should talk with the teacher to discuss how they see this approach working between them. Starting with an open dialog about the approach and then providing some additional information (i.e., samples of this chapter) allows the supervisor and teacher to be on the same page.

The second tip is to establish a timeline of events that works for both individuals. This should be discussed, but it should also be written down so that the supervisor and teacher are both aware of what they need to do and when they need to do it. The supervisor should not dictate the meeting times and when to provide lesson plans. These should be negotiated and should work for both the supervisor and teacher. If one person feels overwhelmed by the time commitment, or feels pressure, the experience will not be positive. The supervisor and teacher should reserve one hour for the one-on-one conversation. A longer conversation is not productive. Less than an hour can make the conversation feel rushed. If everything has not been discussed during the hour, and the supervisor feels that they are being productive, then the supervisor should ask if there is another day or time when they can meet again. Respecting each other's time is crucial.

The final tip to make both types of oral feedback successful is for the supervisor to follow up with the teacher in person. Since a major benefit is that both approaches create an opportunity for a teacher and supervisor to meet and have a professional conversation about a teacher's practice, the follow-up should be in person to continue that professional relationship. The follow-up should be informal to reduce any risk that the teacher would feel as though he/she is being monitored or evaluated.

For the *Lesson Plan Walk Through*, the supervisor should stop by the teacher's classroom after the lesson was taught and simply ask, "How did the lesson go?" This question leaves it open and allows the teacher space to reflect. The supervisor might follow up by asking, "Be honest, did our discussion help?" These two questions open a dialog.

For the *Compare and Contrast*, the supervisor should stop by the classroom about a week after the feedback session and ask the teacher, "Have you been able to implement those goals in your lesson planning?" If the teacher says "Yes," the supervisor can follow up by asking, "Be honest, how is it going?" Again, these questions can continue the conversation that was started and demonstrate to the teacher that the supervisor is interested.

At the end of the follow-up conversation, the supervisor should always ask, "Is there any way I can help?" This shows that the supervisor is willing to provide support. For the follow-up conversation to be authentic and allow the teacher to be honest, the supervisor must be genuine when asking the questions.

Providing oral feedback to teachers about their lesson planning can have impact on their instructional practices, build their professionalism, and create a collaborative working environment between supervisors and teachers. However, both parties must approach it with those goals in mind and believe the other person has the same intentions. That will make the oral feedback experience successful.

4

COMBINATION OF WRITTEN AND ORAL FEEDBACK ON LESSON PLANS

RATIONALE

Teacher candidates and teachers, both novice and experienced, will be evaluated and given feedback throughout their professional career. Performance evaluations (testing) linking student performance to instruction has become more common. Instructional evaluation usually has three components: pre-conferences, observation, and post-conference. Performance evaluations are not designed to be learning experiences; the goal of these evaluations is to rate teachers' effectiveness through student performance and teacher instruction.

Performance evaluations, whether good or bad, are a reality for many teachers. The problem with these high-stakes evaluation measures is that they are not designed to be learning experiences from which teachers to get feedback and improve their practice. This chapter responds to this by providing two strategies that are designed to use lesson planning as a learning experience that will help teachers be successful on performance evaluations.

There are two strategies described in this chapter. Both use writing and oral feedback, and both are the most time-consuming and comprehensive strategies. The first strategy is the *Three-Prong Lesson Reflection*, which uses both oral and written feedback in a pre-conference, observation and post-conference experience, all centered on lesson planning. The second strategy is the *Assessment Driven Lesson Plan*, which focuses on the assessment aspect of how a teacher plans lesson and uses assessment data to drive how he/she writes assessment into the lesson plan.

One of the goals of the combination approach is to prepare teachers (especially novice teachers) with a similar experience to what they will participate in during a performance evaluation. However, the aim of these strategies is not just to give the experience but also to use both oral and written feedback on lesson plans as an educative tool that will impact their teacher practice, and in turn potentially improve how they perform on evaluation measures.

Strategy 5: *Three-Prong Lesson Reflection*

Description of Strategy

The *Three-Prong Lesson Reflection* is designed to have teachers write a lesson plan and provide the rationale behind what they are doing, and then reflect on those decisions. The goal is to have teachers think through the process of planning and preparing for instruction and to use that process to inform future lessons. Most teacher evaluation conferences are designed to have a pre-conference, observation, and post-conference. However, this strategy is about lesson planning and preparation. The *Three-Prong Lesson Reflection* includes (1) preparation, (2) pre-conference, and (3) post-conference.

I. Preparation

Before the pre-conference, the teacher must write a full lesson plan. The lesson plan should follow the school, district, or teacher education program format. Using that lesson plan, the teacher must select three of the five reflection questions to answer. The answers must be written and submitted with the lesson plan to the supervisor at least two days before instruction.

Reflection Questions (select 3)

1. Which part of the lesson plan was the most challenging to write? Why?

2. Which part of the lesson plan was the easiest to write? Why?
3. How do your learning objectives and standards connect to your assessment(s)?
4. What types of learners are you meeting in this lesson plan? Why did you select those learners?

Once the teacher has submitted the lesson and reflection questions, the supervisor must read over and provide written feedback directly on the lesson plan. The written feedback must be in response to the three questions the teacher answered for the reflection piece. For each of the questions answered, the supervisor should provide the following written feedback and send it back to the teacher to review before the pre-conference.

Written feedback on reflection question 1 or 2. If the teacher answered reflection questions 1 and/or 2, the supervisor must go to that part of the lesson plan. The supervisor must read it and give at least one positive comment about it regarding content, pedagogy, or classroom management. Then the supervisor must give at least one comment on something the teacher could think about, add, or change for that section of the lesson plan. The suggestion comment should focus on content, pedagogy, or classroom management.

Written feedback on reflection question 3. Assessments should clearly align to the learning objectives and standards that guide the lesson. This question challenges a teacher to think about how those two parts of a lesson plan connect. After reading the teacher's response, the supervisor should write comments under the assessment section of the lesson plan.

First, the supervisor should write a note next to each assessment identifying which of the objectives and/or standards the assessment addresses. Next, the supervisor should write if there is any assessment written that doesn't have a corresponding learning objective or standard, or if there is a learning objective or standard that does not have an assessment. Finally, the supervisor should write one suggestion for an assessment that would be easy to implement within the given lesson plan that might provide the teacher with some understanding of student content knowledge. The supervisor should connect it to one or more of the objectives and/or standards.

Written feedback on reflection question 4. This question is designed to have teachers reflect on how they are differentiating their instruction to accommodate different learners in the classroom. The goal is not to have a teacher write a lesson that meets every different type of learner. The goal of this question is to have a teacher think critically about whom they are meeting for that particular lesson, and make sure their pedagogical strategies actually match those learners.

The supervisor should read the teacher's reflection, and then provide written feedback. The supervisor should note where in the lesson plan (procedures and assessment sections) there is evidence of meeting those types of learners (i.e., visual, auditory, kinesthetic learners, etc.). The notation on the type(s) of learner(s) being met should be in the margin next to the evidence. If the supervisor sees evidence of meeting a type of learner that the teacher did not identify, the supervisor should also indicate that on the lesson plan.

II. Pre-Conference

Before the teacher implements the lesson, the teacher and supervisor must meet to discuss the lesson plan, reflections, and written feedback. The pre-conference should take about an hour. The supervisor should ask the following four questions:

1. What changes are going to be made to the lesson plan? Why?
2. What still needs to be done in preparation for the lesson?
3. Based on the lesson plan and the feedback, what challenges do you foresee?
4. What outcomes do you expect from this lesson plan?

The questions should be asked sequentially. They mirror questions that a teacher would be expected to answer during a teacher evaluation (i.e., identifying challenges, expected outcomes, etc.). However, the supervisor must keep in mind that this is not a teacher evaluation. The teacher should feel comfortable in asking questions, and the supervisor should use this as a time to mentor and support the teacher. Questions should be answered, but there should be room for the conversation to grow organically.

At the end of the pre-conference, the supervisor should write down what changes the teacher will make to the lesson plan. He/she will also write down the goals of the lesson and challenges they both anticipate. These will be referred to during the post-conference.

III. Post-Conference

For this strategy to work, the supervisor does not need to observe the lesson. However, if the teacher and supervisor want to negotiate that point and have the supervisor observe as another way to model a true teacher evaluation, it is okay to observe the lesson. Regardless of the observation, the supervisor and teacher must have the post-conference within one day of teaching the lesson.

Just like the pre-conference, the post-conference follows a series of sequential questions. The supervisor must ask the questions, and the teacher should respond, but then there can and should be open dialog between both parties.

1. Do you (the teacher) think the students mastered the learning objectives and standards outlined in the lesson plan?
    a. What evidence did you observe or collect to support this claim?
2. Do you (the teacher) believe the implemented lesson aligned to the written lesson?
    a. What aspects were consistent?
    b. Which aspects of the written lesson plan did not align, and why?
3. What challenges arose during instruction?
    a. Do you think there was any way to write something in your lesson plan that would have accommodated for those challenges?
        i. If so, what would that have been?
        ii. If not, why not?

The final piece to the post-conference is having the supervisor give direct feedback. The supervisor should answer the following two questions:

1. If this were a teacher evaluation, where would the teacher stand?
2. What specific teacher practices does the supervisor expect to see in terms of lesson planning, preparation, and implementation of lesson plans as a result of the *Three-Prong Lesson Plan Reflection*?

Strategy 6: *Assessment Driven Lesson Plan*

Description of Strategy

The *Assessment Driven Lesson Plan* approach is designed to have the teacher write the lesson plan using data to inform what and how he/she will teach. The teacher will receive both oral and written feedback throughout the process. The process contains three parts: (1) Initial Planning Conference (oral feedback), (2) Writing Cycle (written feedback), (3) Instruction and (4) Post-Assessment Conference (oral feedback).

I. Initial Planning Conference (Oral Feedback)

The *Assessment Driven Lesson Plan* strategy is the only approach in which the teacher and supervisor develop the lesson plan together. Before the teacher begins writing the lesson plan, the teacher and supervisor meet to discuss student data in an initial planning conference. The *Assessment Driven Lesson Plan* strategy is the only approach in which the teacher does not write the lesson plan before meeting with the supervisor.

For the initial planning conference, the teacher or supervisor should come prepared with student data. If the supervisor wants to train the teacher on how to use high-stakes testing data to plan for instruction, than the supervisor must prepare that student data for the meeting. Otherwise, the teacher can bring student data.

If the teacher brings student data, the data should be quantified data based on student work connected to content understanding. For example, data could come from a chapter exam/quiz. Results from the exam should be an overall score as well as a breakdown of the score based on the skills/concepts covered in the exam. Data could be students' performance on a writing sample using desegregated scores from a rubric. The data must provide quantitative information on students' understanding of content parceled about by skill/concept.

Table 4.1 provides examples of quantitative data of five students' performance on a spelling test.

Column marked Student Group 1 represents students' overall scores. This data would not be sufficient because it does not provide enough information about the skills or concepts. "Student Group 2" is also from a spelling test, but Dara is parceled out by skill. The type of data from Group 2 would be sufficient for a supervisor and teacher to have a robust initial planning conference.

Table 4.1 Quantified Data of Students' Performance on a Spelling Test

Student Group 1 (Overall Score)		***Student Group 2 (Desegregated Scores)***			
Student ID	*Overall Score on Spelling Exam (out of 10)*	*Student ID*	*Got all 5 prefix words correct (1=yes; 0=no)*	*Got all 5 suffix words correct (1=yes; 0=no)*	*Overall Score on Spelling Exam (out of 10)*
Student A	9	Student V	0	0	8
Student B	9	Student W	1	1	10
Student C	7	Student X	1	0	8
Student D	6	Student Y	0	0	5
Student E	10	Student Z	1	1	10

The initial planning conference must focus on three general questions about content, pedagogy, and classroom management. The supervisor should ask a series of questions and allow the teacher to answer the questions using the data. The supervisor should participate in answering the questions to help give ideas or further challenge a teacher.

1. Content Questions
    a. Using the data, what skills/concepts do students understand?
    b. What skills/concepts are being developed?
    c. What skills/concepts do students struggle to understand?
2. Classroom Management/Grouping Students
    a. What are different ways to group students (small groups, partners, half the class, etc.)?
    b. If put in those groups, what specific skills/concepts would be covered in each group?
3. Pedagogical Practices
    a. What different activities could you do in class to cover those skills/concepts (brainstorm)?
    b. Which activities connect best to the ways you want to group students?

The questions should be asked and answered, but the questions might spur additional conversation. The supervisor must be flexible in terms of the conference and allow the conversation to grow.

The initial planning conference should take about an hour. This should be done a couple of days prior to teaching the lesson so the teacher has sufficient time to go through the writing-cycle process (writing the lesson and receiving feedback), and to prepare materials before instruction.

At the conference, the teacher and supervisor should write down an outline/sketch of the lesson plan. It should include what will be taught (learning objectives and standards). Some general ideas of the learning activities (procedures) and ideas about how student understand will be evaluated during the lesson (assessment). The lesson plan format should be one selected by the school, district, or teacher education program. If a format is not in place, then the supervisor and teacher should outline a format before the initial planning conference concludes.

II. Writing Cycle (Written Feedback)

After the initial planning conference, the teacher must write out a full detailed lesson plan using the outline he/she constructed with the supervisor. This part of the strategy is called the *writing cycle* because it will go back and forth between the teacher and supervisor.

The teacher will write the lesson plan. Once it is complete, it is given to the supervisor. The supervisor will read the lesson plan, using an assessment lens. First, the supervisor will read the learning objectives and standards. For each of those items, the supervisor will check the assessment section of the lesson plan to see if there is a corresponding assessment. If there is, the supervisor will put a checkmark (or some form of notation) next to the objective and/or standard to designate that it has some way of being evaluated. If the objective and/or standard does not have a clear corresponding assessment, then it is highlighted to indicate to the teacher that it needs to have a way of being evaluated.

Second, the supervisor will review just the assessment section. If there were any assessments written that did not have a corresponding objective or standard, then the supervisor should highlight it. Then the supervisor should go through each assessment and indicate what type of data would be collected (i.e., qualitative, quantitative, subjective, objective, student reported, etc.). This is to see what type of data is being collected.

Next, the supervisor goes through the procedures section of the lesson plan to pinpoint where in the lesson the teacher is doing each form of assessment. One suggestion is to number or letter each type of assessment, and then put the corresponding number/letter next to the procedure. Keep in mind; one assessment might be evaluated multiple times in a lesson. Each time it is being evaluated, it must be identified in the procedures. The goal is to identify when in a lesson the teacher is assessing students.

If the supervisor thinks an assessment is being covered, but it is not clearly described, he/she should make some special notation. This is to indicate it to the teacher, so that it can be clearly included in the rewrite.

Finally, the supervisor needs to provide clear feedback for the teacher. The feedback for this strategy focuses on three questions. Depending on the answers, the supervisor must give real suggestions for what a teacher could do. Unlike other strategies, the feedback given from the supervisor to the teacher is actual suggestions and ideas that the teacher can implement. This is only because this strategy is designed to have the supervisor and teacher collaborate at the beginning of the lesson plan process. So it is a collaborative effort.

The supervisor must take the time to write out short, but clear, answers to each of the following three feedback questions:

1. Do all the objectives and standards have corresponding assessments? If no, the supervisor must include one or two suggestions for assessments that could easily be incorporated into the lesson. These suggestions must also indicate what type of assessment data is being collected (i.e., qualitative, quantitative, etc.).
2. Are all the assessments clearly incorporated into the lesson? If no, the supervisor must include one or two suggestions for ways to incorporate each assessment that is not already included.
3. For each assessment, what information you think the data will provide?

The lesson plan with the assessment notations and the short answers to the feedback questions must be given back to the teacher. The teacher takes the written feedback and revises the lesson plan. The teacher must address any missing objective, standard, or assessment. The teacher does not need to incorporate any or all of the suggestions given by the supervisor but must address all missing points. Once revisions have been made, the teacher must give a copy to the supervisor before instruction.

III. INSTRUCTION

The supervisor may choose to observe the lesson, but it is not a requirement for this strategy. The teacher and supervisor should discuss if the supervisor will observe. If the supervisor does observe, he/she should be given a job to help the teacher by collecting some type of data that is part of the assessments for the lesson plan.

If the supervisor is not observing the lesson, the teacher must still plan on collecting student work based on the assessments written in the lesson. The teacher should not do anything with the data until the post-assessment conference. During that time, the supervisor and teacher will review and analyze the work collected.

IV. Post Assessment Conference (Oral Feedback)

Immediately following instruction (within one day), the supervisor and teacher should meet for the post-assessment conference. The intention of the conference is to review student work that was collected. Not all work will be reviewed; the supervisor and teacher can decide together which of the assessment pieces from the lesson plan should be analyzed together.

Remember, the conference is not a teacher evaluation; instead, it is a learning opportunity. The supervisor should encourage the teacher to review a form of assessment that might pose challenges or provide more information about student learning.

Together the teacher and supervisor should take student work and find a way to quantify student learning based on skills and concepts. The data should be organized and categorized to make it easy to come to some conclusions—similar to the data they reviewed before planning the lesson.

Once the data has been organized, the supervisor should ask a series of questions about students who demonstrated understanding of the material, students who still need support, and the overall use of assessments for future lessons.

Series of Questions:

1. Which students mastered the learning objective and/or standard?
   a. What is the data to support your response?
   b. What is the next step for those students?

2. Which students still need help understanding the objective and/or standard?
   a. What is the data to support your response?
   b. What specifically do you want to do with those students to provide the necessary support?
3. Reflect on the overall experience of connecting assessments to objectives/standards and to the procedures section of the lesson plan.
   a. Do you think reviewing student data prior to planning helped with your planning and instruction? In what ways?
   b. This was an intense process; how can the process be incorporate into your daily planning and preparation?

The questions should be answered by the teacher, but with support and feedback from the supervisor. It should be a conversation. The aim is to use real student work to inform a teacher's planning and then together discuss data that represents the lesson that was taught.

The supervisor needs to share what he/she should say or the type of feedback he/she would give if this student data were a form of teacher evaluation. This will be helpful for a teacher to hear, so he/she knows what to expect when an evaluation occurs.

At the end of the conference, the supervisor and teacher should review the goals of this strategy and use the outcomes of this experience to set future planning goals for the teacher.

COMBINATION APPROACH BENEFITS, DRAWBACKS, AND TIPS

There are multiple benefits associated with the combination of written and oral feedback. The main benefit is that the strategies outlined in this chapter provide experiences that a teacher would participate in during a formal teacher evaluation.

As with the evaluation model, the supervisor has a clear set of questions and guidelines. For teacher evaluations, supervisors are often given a set of questions and procedures to follow. The aim is to reduce the risk of favoritism or giving special preference to one teacher over another. These strategies provide a similar scenario. The supervisor is given a set of questions to be used during the conferences. The teacher is also given a set of instructions or reflection questions.

A supervisor might use one or both approaches with teachers in the school to model the evaluation. This way, all teachers have a similar experience by receiving the same set of questions and instructions. The difference is in the conversations that take place and the written feedback. These strategies provide the same type of evaluation experience, but allow a space for the supervisor to differentiate the feedback and learning experience based on individual needs of each teacher.

While the other strategies in this book are for novice teachers, these two strategies can be used with any teacher at any stage in their teaching. Since teachers are constantly being evaluated, and there is an aspect of these approaches that tailors the feedback to individual teachers, the combination approach can work for a range of teacher experiences.

One of the benefits of the combination approach is that the teacher receives both oral and written feedback, but the drawback is the time commitment. Both strategies are time sensitive. They require a lot to happen from both the supervisor and teacher in a relatively short period.

For example, once the teacher writes and submits the lesson plan, the written feedback, pre-conference, instruction, and post-conference all happen within a three-day period. The *Assessment Driven Lesson Plan* has a little more flexibility with time; the pre-conference to discuss the lesson plan can happen a couple of days before the actual lesson. However, the turn-around time for providing written feedback on the lesson plan and then meeting after instruction to review student work is relatively short.

For either strategy to work and be successful, both the supervisor and teacher must be willing and able to provide ample time. Both parties should look at their calendar and make sure they can give the necessary time during that period. If not, the supervisor or teacher might want to suggest a different strategy. Or if they want to do one of the combination approaches, they should look ahead at a week that is less demanding that both can commit to. For it to be successful, both parties should feel comfortable with giving ample time.

If there is a challenge in finding time for the teacher to meet during school hours, the supervisor might be able to have other teachers help. Since one of the benefits of the combination approach is to have a supervisor implement it with a group of teachers at a school, there might be a way to coordinate some relief time to help assist with the post-conference.

Since these approaches model an evaluation, experienced teachers, mentor teachers, or teachers who are interested in pursuing administration or supervision could be assigned to implement the strategy with a novice teacher. If a principal or supervisor does not have time, these approaches can be used in a mentor-mentee relationship.

Another tip for making these strategies work is for clear communication between both parties prior to engaging in either strategy. One of the benefits of these strategies is that they provide an evaluation experience to a teacher without actually evaluating the teacher. However, there is a fine line between providing clear and direct written and oral feedback to challenge and change a teacher's practices in a positive manner and providing feedback that comes across as judgmental.

This often is due to miscommunication or a lack of understanding. The supervisor should clearly communicate the strategy prior to engaging and ask if this is something the teacher would want to do. If the teacher does not feel comfortable at the beginning, he/she might become very defensive in the process. The supervisor should also explain the goal of the approach and reiterate throughout the process that it is not an evaluation and is only being used as a learning tool.

To reduce the risk of the strategies being used incorrectly, the supervisor and teacher should develop a relationship in which they feel comfortable working together—where they both understand where the other is coming from and how the other responds to different situations (see chapter 5). By developing a working relationship prior to engaging in either strategy, these approaches will more likely be successful and become a positive learning experience.

5

FOUR CASE STUDIES

USING CASE STUDIES TO DEVELOP A PROFESSIONAL RELATIONSHIP

Before a supervisor starts providing oral or written feedback on lesson plans, the supervisor (principal, administrator, cooperating teacher, host teacher, teacher educator, etc.) and mentee (teacher, novice teacher, student teacher, field student, etc.) should engage in an experience to develop a common understanding of how each person thinks about giving and receiving feedback. What works and does not work for both the supervisor and mentee is important for the other person to know. Understanding how each party thinks and feels about feedback is necessary for establishing procedures for how the relationship will work.

The following four cases should be used to begin a dialog between both parties. Each case represents a situation between a supervisor and mentee that is linked to lesson planning. Although each case represents a different type of relationship, all four cases are applicable to any supervisor and mentee relationship. Each case can and should be used by any supervisor and mentee planning to engage in providing and receiving feedback on lesson plans.

Cases are written in the same format. To begin, a narrative of the case is presented. The narratives originate from true events, which have been modified for the purposes of this book. All names have been changed. The narratives should be read by both the supervisor and mentee independently.

Following the narrative is a reflection section. Both parties must answer a series of three to five reflection questions. The supervisor and mentee will have a different set of questions. The reflection questions are designed to make the supervisor and mentee think about actions and solutions they would take if they were put in a similar situation. The questions should be fully answered by each person independently.

After answering the questions, the supervisor and mentee should come together for the discussion. The discussion section should be read together. Clear directions are provided for how the conversation should start and what each person should share from his/her reflections. This initiates the conversation, and both the teacher and supervisor should allow room for the conversation to develop organically and continue. Each discussion section is very different and aligns to the case. The discussions are also different so that a supervisor and mentee may do all four cases, and will have very different discussions.

Before the conversation concludes, both the supervisor and mentee should establish procedures for how they would enter the relationship for giving and receiving feedback that works for both of them and also for establishing what does not work for them. This will help establish norms for the relationship to be successful.

To conclude the conversation, the supervisor and mentee should read the last section ("Suggestions from the Author") together. This section provides an overview of how the author interpreted this case and suggestions for how to think about lesson planning and providing meaningful feedback in a difficult situation. This might spur more conversation between the supervisor and mentee, which is good and should be encouraged.

Once the supervisor and mentee have read and discussed the cases, both the supervisor and mentee should establish procedures for how they would enter the relationship for giving and receiving feedback that works for both of them regardless of the case or scenario and establishing what does not work for them. This will help ensure the relationship is successful, and the feedback is provided and received in a positive manner with good intentions to improve teacher practice.

The goal of these cases is to provide four scenarios in which supervisors and mentees are forced to think about their role in this relationship, and discuss what works for them and what might be frustrating. Using cases to open this dialog and establish routines that work for both people is important for the success of providing feedback on lesson plans.

CASE 1: THE STUDENT TEACHER WHO KNEW IT ALL

Narrative

Mrs. Benji hosted a field student for reading practicum every semester. She thought it was great to have extra help in her class. It gave students individual reading instruction. She always prepared reading centers to coincide with the field student. Each week, she would tell the field student the reading skill that the children would be working on the following week and provide some general information and resources to align with the skill. The field student would take that information and develop a mini-lesson to implement with a small reading group.

On the day of the lesson, the field student would bring in a copy of the lesson plan. Mrs. Benji would quickly review it and provide verbal feedback. Suggestions of things the field student might not have considered were based on what she reviewed from the lesson plan. For example, if the lesson included reading vocabulary, Mrs. Benji might ask if the field student had definitions and examples to help clarify words for students. Mrs. Benji wanted to mentor field students by giving ideas and suggestions based on what they had already constructed for their lesson without dictating what they should or should not do.

Mrs. Benji did not directly communicate to field students her expectations for the mini-lesson plan, or how she would provide feedback. However, it always worked out. Mrs. Benji felt it happened naturally, and she always felt good about the professional relationships she built with field students.

The university contacted Mrs. Benji and asked if she would host a student teacher. She was hesitant because she had already committed to having a weekly field student for reading, and she never mentored a student teacher before. She knew it would be a lot different from hosting a field student. However, with some encouragement from her principal and the college, she agreed.

Andrea was assigned to Mrs. Benji. On the first day, she was up helping students and being proactive in setting up materials and pulling resources. Mrs. Benji told Andrea that she was impressed by her attitude and ability to see what needed to be done and then did it. Mrs. Benji was surprised the following day when Andrea interrupted her during math to tell students to get out their homework so she could check it. That was not how Mrs. Benji reviewed homework, but she let it go.

As days and weeks progressed, Andrea continued to interrupt and give classroom management directions to students. Mrs. Benji wanted Andrea participating, but she thought it should have been discussed ahead of time because some of Andrea's directions did not match Mrs. Benji's instructional practices. Mrs. Benji tried to have a conversation with Andrea, and asked Andrea what her rationale was for giving certain instructions. Each time Mrs. Benji asked her, Andrea responded by saying it was what she learned in class, and it was best practice. Mrs. Benji thought Andrea's rationale was very vague. She also thought it was a little insulting, implying that she did not use best practices.

Mrs. Benji noticed that every time she asked Andrea her rationale for doing something, Andrea would become very defensive. Andrea would provide a quick answer, and the conversation would end. There was no dialog about her teaching practices.

As time continued, there were three events that caused Mrs. Benji to reconsider if hosting Andrea was the best idea. The first problem was when Andrea told the students to go to the carpet for a read aloud. Mrs. Benji wanted them to stay at their desks because she had prepared a writing activity to accompany the read aloud. She was planning to use the doc camera to read and show the book, and have students at their desks so they could write. Having Andrea interrupt and tell students to go to the carpet meant they needed clipboards, pencils, and worksheets. Students would have to negotiate space at the carpet to write. When asked about Andrea's rationale, she quickly said that all read alouds are supposed to be at the carpet and that Mrs. Benji should allow students to learn in different spaces around the room, not always at their desks.

The second problem arose during reading centers. The field student provided a lesson to Mrs. Benji, and they discussed it before class. Mrs.

Benji asked to see Andrea's lesson; Andrea said she did not believe she needed to write a mini-lesson plan just for a center. That was something field students should do, but for student teaching she was more advanced.

During centers, Andrea did not cover the reading skill Mrs. Benji asked her to go over, and she also finished early and told students to go back to their desks and silent read. Mrs. Benji felt this was a time students got individual reading support. She did not want students reading independently. On the other hand, the field student provided a mini-lesson, and Mrs. Benji gave feedback. The field student applied the feedback during centers and did a great job covering the reading skill and working with the students.

The final incident occurred when Andrea asked to take over a full subject. Mrs. Benji was hesitant, but agreed. Mrs. Benji said she could lead science class the following week and gave Andrea the science topic, skills, and resources to use. She asked Andrea if she had any questions or wanted to discuss the content and possible activities. Andrea declined, saying she had ideas. Mrs. Benji did not push to have a conversation, but asked Andrea to write the lessons ahead of time so she could review them.

A day before the unit began, Andrea came prepared with a series of lesson plans. Mrs. Benji read through the lessons and started asking questions about Andrea's rationale of why she decided to do certain things. Mrs. Benji was asking questions to challenge Andrea to think about the rationale behind her decisions for teaching certain content using certain methods. Andrea became very defensive and told Mrs. Benji that she just wanted to try the unit without discussing it first. She wanted Mrs. Benji to trust her.

Mrs. Benji watched the introductory lesson. She noticed that Andrea had a lot of confidence in leading the class. She was very clear giving directions and leading students through the activity. The problem was that the content was not well developed and students would ask content-specific questions that Andrea could not answer. The activity was superficial and did not advance students' understanding of the content. The lesson went well, but Mrs. Benji thought the content and pedagogical practices needed to be improved.

Working with field students, Mrs. Benji always felt good about having an open dialog. She usually used lesson plans before instruction to begin a conversation. However, every time she tried to have a conversation with Andrea about content, pedagogy, or other teaching practices, Andrea became defensive. This was not the type of professional relationship Mrs. Benji wanted, and she did not know what to do. She wanted Andrea to become a great teacher, not just an okay one. Mrs. Benji knew that with support, she could help Andrea develop, but she did not know how to initiate the conversation.

Reflection

Before discussing Mrs. Benji and Andrea's situation, the supervisor and mentee must reflect on individual questions. The supervisor will reflect on questions about what Mrs. Benji did and develop suggestions about what Mrs. Benji could do moving forward. The supervisor will also think about how it might apply to his/her own supervision style. The mentee will reflect on similar questions, but from Andrea's point of view, thinking about why Andrea might have responded in a defensive manner, and applying that to how they might respond to feedback. After each person reflects independently, both the supervisor and mentee should come together for the discussion section.

Reflection Questions for the Supervisor

1. What did Mrs. Benji do that were good supervision practices? Which of these practices align to how you supervise?
2. What did Mrs. Benji do that might be been problematic for supervision? Do those align to your own supervision practices?
3. If you were in Mrs. Benji's situation, what specific actions would you take to build a relationship and dialog with Andrea? Why do those specific actions (practices) work for you?
4. If you were to help Andrea by using a lesson-planning feedback strategy, which strategy would you use? Why?

Reflection Questions for the Mentee

1. What mistakes do you think Andrea made? Why do you think Andrea responded to Mrs. Benji the way she did?

2. What type of supervision situations make you respond in a defensive manner? Why?
3. In this situation, which type of lesson-planning feedback strategy do you think would work for Andrea? Why?
4. Would that strategy work for you? What specific actions would you need from your supervisor to make it work?

Discussion

Before discussing solutions for Mrs. Benji and Andrea, it is important that the supervisor and mentee use the case as a way to discuss methods for supervision that align with their own personalities. Not all reflection questions will be directly addressed in the following discussion, but thinking through those questions will be helpful.

To begin, the mentee should share his/her answers to reflection questions 1 and 2. These questions identify personality traits of Andrea and have the mentee reflect on how he/she might respond to supervision situations. The supervisor may ask questions to learn more about the mentee and what works and does not work for the mentee. This will help the supervisor think about how he/she might engage the mentee so the supervision relationship is positive.

The supervisor should then share answers to reflection questions 1, 2, and 3. Since the mentee had a chance to share, it is important that the supervisor also gets to share methods for how he/she supervises and why those methods work for him/her. Oftentimes, there are good reasons for why a supervisor uses a method or acts a certain way, but without communicating that to the mentee, it can come across as judgmental. Sharing how a supervisor provides support and how a mentee responds to supervision through this case study will open communication between both parties.

After they share how each responds to supervision, the discussion should open up to the case. Both the supervisor and mentee should openly share what they thought about Mrs. Benji and Andrea. Together, the supervisor and mentee should discuss what they thought Mrs. Benji did right and the mistakes she made. They should do the same for Andrea. By discussing what these characters did right, wrong, and should do differently, the supervisor and mentee can begin applying their findings to their own professional relationship.

Finally, the supervisor and mentee must answer the following two questions about how lesson plan feedback might be a solution to this case, and how it could be applied to their own style of supervision. After the questions have been answered, the supervisor and mentee should read the next section, "Suggestions from the Author."

1. In this situation, which strategy for lesson plan feedback would you suggestion to Mrs. Benji and Andrea? Why?
2. Would that strategy work for both of you?
   a. If this would work for you, what specific procedures do you need in place to make it successful?
   b. If it would not work, what challenges are associated with this strategy that would not make it work for your style of giving or receiving feedback?

Suggestions from the Author

This narrative was about Mrs. Benji, who did a good job mentoring field students but never thought through her mentoring practices and did not communicate her methods. Mrs. Benji's methods might have been good and might have worked for many mentees. However, Mrs. Benji never communicated those methods, and when put in a challenging situation, the lack of communication caused misunderstandings that led to a breakdown in giving and receiving feedback. Supervisors must be able to identify methods they are using for supervision and their rationale for those methods and then be able to communicate that information to the mentee.

In a supervisor and mentee relationship in which the mentee is defensive or takes feedback personally, open communication can be stunted. A beneficial strategy for providing oral feedback post-instruction would be *Compare and Contrast* (see chapter 3). For one thing, the strategy forces both parties to talk. In a situation like Mrs. Benji and Andrea's, the supervisor does not want to select a written feedback strategy because it would not force dialog. Mrs. Benji and Andrea need to work on their communication, and using an oral feedback approach would help do that.

Second, selecting a strategy that reduces subjectivity might also reduce a mentee's defensive reactions. Andrea was very defensive and wanted Mrs. Benji to trust her decisions. For this strategy, Mrs. Benji would only use the written lesson plan to help her record the instruction. Andrea would be responsible for analyzing how her lesson plan compared to and contrasted with her instruction. She would lead the discussion, and Mrs. Benji's suggestions would be solely based on what Andrea identified. Since the challenges and areas that needed improvement would not be initiated by Mrs. Benji, it could reduce Andrea's defensiveness.

Do not mistake this strategy as only working for mentees who are defensive or supervisors who lack communication. Providing oral feedback post-instruction is a great way to build communication between the supervisor and mentee in a positive and professional manner. It also helps give a mentee confidence in leading the discussion and analyzing his/her own practice.

CASE 2: THE EXPERIENCED TEACHER WHO DOESN'T LESSON PLAN

Narrative

James was starting his student teaching experience. He had been in classrooms for other teacher education courses, but this would be different. He would be with the same class with the same head teacher every day, all day, for an entire semester. He would get to know the different curricula and textbooks used, design a full unit of study, and implement it. It would be his chance to take all the tools and teacher practices he developed in teacher education and apply them.

James had been assigned to Mrs. Frizzle. He heard great things about her. Mrs. Frizzle had been teaching for twenty years in the district. She had taught a range of grades and subjects and in schools within the same district. For the past ten years, she had been working at High Hills Elementary teaching third grade. The principal and parents liked her because she was able to challenge her students and get a lot of growth from them academically during one school year.

When James and Mrs. Frizzle met for the first time, she described her method for hosting student teachers. She did not believe a student teacher should sit back and observe. She wanted James up on his feet helping students on the first day. She wanted James to get to know the kids. Mrs. Frizzle said the most important aspect of student teaching was what he did during instructional time, working directly with students one-on-one, in small groups, and with the whole class.

During planning time (non-instructional time), she wanted James to grade papers and provide meaningful feedback on all student work. She asked James to keep records, based on student homework and classwork, of how students were mastering different skills for each subject and unit of study. Mrs. Frizzle showed James how she kept track of all that information. She said she used that information to help guide her instruction (data-driven instruction) and to have conversations with parents about student progress.

James was very impressed and could tell he would learn a lot about instructional practices and data-driven instruction. After having a great conversation, he asked Mrs. Frizzle about writing lesson plans and writing a full unit plan to implement during his student teaching. Mrs. Frizzle told him that teachers really do not lesson plan, and that she would not ask to see his lesson plans. She did not want to force him to do extra work that she believed teachers really did not do. James was surprised since he spent so much time in teacher education developing lesson plans, but he was thrilled because it would save him a lot of time.

The beginning of student teaching was great. James followed Mrs. Frizzle's lead. He copied her style of instruction and learned a lot about collecting data, and what that data told him about students. During lunch and prep time, Mrs. Frizzle and James worked very hard to prepare the materials for upcoming lessons, and they talked extensively about what they would be teaching, and about the students. They had developed a positive professional relationship.

Mrs. Frizzle would leave school right after the bell each day to pick up her own children from school. She would often take work home with her. The work included grading student work, reading materials, and so on. Sometimes she would give some of that work to James. She would tell him that a teacher's work day often continued at home into the evening.

About a month into teaching, Mrs. Frizzle asked James to take the lead for teaching science. She showed him her calendar, which had notes jotted down for each day. The notes included the topic that would be covered and an idea for an activity. His unit would be about weather. For the first day, she wrote in her calendar "weather, look at the sky, and journal."

James struggled on the first day of the unit on weather. There was no science content, and students' journal entries were superficial. In addition to the dearth of science content, James did not develop any science skills or writing skills. A lesson Mrs. Frizzle would spend thirty minutes delivering, James finished in ten minutes. Students were off task. It was not a good lesson.

James knew it was not a good first lesson. During prep time, he asked Mrs. Frizzle what he could do to make it better, and she told him that it was probably first-day nerves. She suggested that he relax, look at her calendar for the content and suggested activity for the next day, and then copy how she taught other subjects and try to apply that type of instructional delivery.

The following lesson was worse. The lesson did not have strong content, and the activity did not match the content that he was supposed to cover. There was no formative assessment being collected on students' content or skill development. His time management was off, and as a result students were disengaged.

Mrs. Frizzle and James kept talking about different ideas during lunch and prep time. She even sent him e-mails at night when she was home, when she was thinking about what he could do to improve. She wanted to stay positive and help him. James was great at supporting Mrs. Frizzle's instruction for the other subjects throughout the day, but he continued to struggle when it came to his own lessons.

When Mrs. Frizzle asked James's college supervisor for some ideas, the supervisor asked to see James's lesson plans. Mrs. Frizzle explained that teachers do not lesson plan, so she felt it would be a waste to require student teachers to engage in a practice they would not do as a practicing teacher.

Reflection

Before the supervisor and mentee discuss James and Mrs. Frizzle, both parties must answer the following set of questions designed for their individual roles. Only after answering the questions independently, the teacher and supervisor should come together for the discussion section.

Reflection Questions for the Supervisor

1. Think about your own experience in teacher preparation courses, student teaching, the first year of teaching, the second year of teaching, and your current teaching. Reflecting on those five time periods, describe how you lesson planned during each of those five periods of time.
2. Looking across your descriptions of how you lesson planned, how did your practice of lesson planning change over time?
   a. If your practice for lesson planning changed, what were the different variables that you believe contributed to that change?
   b. If your practice for lesson planning stayed the same, why do you think it remained constant?
3. If you were Mrs. Frizzle, what lesson plan feedback strategy would you try to use with James, and why?

Reflection Questions for the Mentee

1. What are the most challenging aspects of lesson planning for you, and why? What parts of lesson planning do you think are the most helpful for you, and why?
2. Has lesson planning ever improved your content, pedagogy, and/or classroom management?
   a. If yes, describe specific lessons you created and how they impacted your content, pedagogy, and/or classroom management.
   b. If no, think of a current lesson plan or a lesson you taught that did not go well. What content, pedagogy, and classroom management directions could have been added to that lesson plan? Be specific.
3. If you were James, which strategy for lesson plan feedback would you want to try implementing with Mrs. Frizzle, and why?

Discussion

For this case, the discussion should begin with the supervisor sharing his/her answers to reflection questions 1 and 2. (Please save the final question for later.) These questions provide an opportunity for a supervisor to share his/her own experiences lesson planning and how lesson planning has changed in his/her professional career over time. Having the mentee hear this story will help them understand that a teacher's lesson planning changes over time.

While the supervisor is sharing, the mentee should ask questions to gain more information. For instance, if the supervisor shares that district policies have influenced how he/she currently lesson plans, the mentee should feel free to ask questions about policies.

After sharing the experience, the mentee should share his/her response to question 1. This question will provide the supervisor an understanding of what is challenging for the mentee and what aspects of lesson planning are helpful. Knowing this information will allow a supervisor to customize how they support their mentee by focusing and helping in areas that are challenging, and then leveraging those aspects of lesson planning that are helpful.

Once the supervisor and mentee have answered and shared those questions, together they should answer the following two questions, which relate to both of their last reflection questions about lesson planning.

1. In this situation, which strategy for providing lesson plan feedback do you think would be beneficial for James and work within the professional relationship between James and Mrs. Frizzle? Why?
2. Would this strategy work for the both of you?
   a. If so, what would you need from each other to make it successful?
   b. If this strategy does not work for you, why not?

Up to this point, the discussion would be about the supervisor's and mentee's lesson plan experiences, how lesson plan feedback could work in this case, and if a certain strategy would work for them. Moving forward, the discussion should be about developing strategies that would work for their professional relationship and establishing norms.

Once this has been discussed, the conversation can open up to be about the actual case and having each person share what they thought about Mrs. Frizzle and James. Having a free and open dialog about the case will help create a common experience around a scenario.

Suggestions from the Author

This case is an example of a master teacher who has a lot of experience, wants to help her student teacher succeed, but does not see lesson planning as a possible strategy. How a teacher lesson plans, and what their lesson plans look like, will change over time (see chapter 1).

Experienced teachers' lesson plans should look different from lesson plans of a novice teacher. However, experienced teachers often forget how their lesson plans have changed and might not have been challenged to think about how or why their lesson plans have adapted. The reflection questions for the supervisor and discussion section were specifically designed to challenge a supervisor to think about this issue, and share their experience.

Novice teachers need to recognize that developing their teacher practice takes time and work. Just because an experienced teacher does or does not do something does not mean it is directly applicable for a novice.

In this situation, Mrs. Frizzle was supportive and encouraging. Mrs. Frizzle did spend the school hours working hard, but she was limited on the additional time she could give to James outside of school hours. Recognizing personal limitations is important, not for judgmental reasons, but to pick strategies that work within a supervisor's and mentee's life. This will help make the overall experience successful.

Because of Mrs. Frizzle's limitations, she would want to select a written feedback strategy. She was willing to do additional work, but finding time to meet was difficult. Allowing Mrs. Frizzle to review lesson plans and provide written feedback would be something she could do on her own time.

James could benefit from either the *Providing Stems* or *Journalistic Approach* strategies for providing written feedback on lesson plans (see chapter 2). *Providing Stems* is a strategy designed to force a novice teacher to think about what they might say or how they might communicate an idea to students. This helps when a struggling teacher needs someone with experience to show how to start the lesson in terms of delivering the content, or thinking about activities, or management approaches. The supervisor can be very specific in how to approach a lesson, and then the novice teacher can use that information to move forward. This strategy works well when you have a novice teacher like James who recognized he needed help and asked for specific ideas to help improve his practice.

This strategy would also work for Mrs. Frizzle who did not want to tell James what to do or how to do it. The stem would be a way for Mrs. Frizzle to focus James and force him to think about specific aspects of the lesson plan and instruction without dictating what to do. A supervisor who has the time, and experience and is encouraging would do well with this strategy.

The *Journalistic Approach* strategy would also work for James and Mrs. Frizzle. The approach is designed to pose questions to challenge novice teachers to think about things they might not have considered based on their lesson plan. Since James and Mrs. Frizzle have a good professional relationship and communicate well during school hours, this type of feedback would work well.

Regardless of which type of written feedback is used, providing feedback before instruction would be imperative for James. When a mentee is able to recognize that there is a problem with his/her instruction, and asks for suggestions to address a problem directly, the supervisor must be willing to provide feedback before instruction. Getting feedback after the lesson only helps a mentee in future lessons. When a mentee, or supervisor, addresses a problem and wants to see solutions and impact on upcoming lessons, the strategy must be one that gives feedback before instruction.

CASE 3: THE TEACHER GOING FOR TENURE

Narrative

Mr. Gittleman had been teaching social studies at Heritage Middle School for two years. He was starting his third year. He knew that if he could just get through the third year, he would be granted tenure.

The students at Heritage Middle School enjoyed Mr. Gittleman's class. He always had fun activities including mock elections, historical role-plays, debates, and much more. It was rare for students to sit back and listen to Mr. Gittleman lecture or just read out of a textbook.

Principal Williamson also enjoyed the class. However, other teachers did not speak highly of Mr. Gittleman and often complained. Principal Williamson did not let other teachers dictate what she thought about each teacher, but she did listen to complaints because she wanted to support her teachers and make it a positive working environment.

During the past two years, Mr. Gittleman taught sixth grade, but the other sixth-grade team teachers complained that he did not want to be a team player. They said that at their team meetings, the teachers would discuss students' performance on reading, writing, and math benchmark assessments. They would try to think of ways that all the disciplines could incorporate the tested skills into instruction. When it got to his turn, Mr. Gittleman would say that he did not teach to the test and that those skills were not the standards he had to cover for social studies.

Principal Williamson was surprised and thought changing Mr. Gittleman to seventh grade with a different team of teachers the year before he became tenured might help his evaluations. The students and parents loved having Mr. Gittleman again, but his new team had the same complaints.

Principal Williamson believed he was a good teacher, but was not sure why he struggled with his colleagues. She also did not understand how Mr. Gittleman did not see connections between tested skills and his own course of study.

One day, Principal Williamson walked into Mr. Gittleman's class while students were preparing for a debate. Students were doing research on computers and writing down their arguments. She watched Mr. Gittleman go to different groups and ask open-ended questions that would challenge students to do some additional research. Principal Williamson could see students were actively participating and that Mr. Gittleman was working well supporting his students. She could see that from the types of questions he asked, the types of research students were doing, and the debate points students were writing.

After class, Principal Williamson asked to talk to Mr. Gittleman in her office. She expressed to him that she was impressed by what she saw. She asked Mr. Gittleman what he thought of the lesson. He responded that he thought it was great because all of the students were engaged. Principal Williamson said she agreed, but asked Mr. Gittleman what evidence he had that students were engaged. He said he did not understand her question, he just knew they were engaged.

Principal Williamson was surprised by his response, and asked Mr. Gittleman to describe what he thought the students learned in terms of content and the skills they applied during that lesson. Mr. Gittleman said he did not understand her question. He said that students were engaged and learning about their research topic.

Mr. Gittleman asked Principal Williamson if there was a problem with his instruction. She said no, but told him she would like to meet again to discuss his planning and instruction since he would be evaluated soon for tenure.

After he left, Principal Williamson was confused. Mr. Gittleman was great in the class and was engaging his students in meaningful activities. She could identify evidence of student engagement and student learning but was concerned that Mr. Gittleman could not.

Principal Williamson could understand why his colleagues were a little frustrated. She believed that if she could help Mr. Gittleman reflect on his practice, identify what he was teaching (content and skills), and connect it to evidence in the classroom, he would be able to have better conversations with his colleagues regarding student learning. The problem was that Mr. Gittleman was close to earning tenure, and she did not know what she could do to help him reflect and simultaneously do well on his tenure evaluations. She knew he was good, and she did not want to lose Mr. Gittleman.

Reflection

After reading the narrative, the supervisor and mentee should reflect on a series of questions. Unlike with the other case studies, the supervisor and mentee have the same set of questions for this case. However, it is still important that both the supervisor and mentee answer each question independently of each other. Once ready, they should read the discussion section together.

Reflection Questions for the Supervisor and Mentee

1. Which type of feedback would you suggest Principal Williamson recommends to Mr. Gittleman? Why?
2. If you were in a similar situation, which type of lesson plan feedback strategy would you want to use? Why?
3. When did you find yourself in a situation in which you felt you were being judged and needed to defend yourself?
   a. How did you handle it? What would you do the same or do differently?
   b. What did you need from your counterpart?

Discussion

The discussion for this case study will begin by having both the supervisor and mentee share their thoughts about each of the reflection questions. The mentee should begin with the first question, sharing his/her thoughts. The supervisor can then contribute.

The supervisor and mentee should move through each question and sub-question in the same format, having the mentee begin and then the supervisor. These questions are designed to get both parties to reflect on the case but then think about their own experiences receiving feedback. By sharing these experiences, it will open insight into how each handles receiving feedback. Some people take feedback very well and do not get defensive at all. Other people hear feedback as challenges and become defensive. Some people see feedback as a good thing, but still become defensive because that is how they respond to questions about their practice.

There is not a right or wrong way. However, both the supervisor and mentee need to know how each responds to feedback so there is no miscommunication or misunderstanding when both parties are participating in the experience.

Once the mentee and supervisor have answered all questions and sub-questions together, they can let the conversation develop. To wrap up the conversation, they should read the suggestions from the author together and provide any last thoughts.

Suggestions from the Author

Before concluding the conversation, the supervisor and mentee should read this section together. After reading the section, both parties can continue the conversation and make any final recommendation for what Principal Williamson and Mr. Gittleman should do. Finally, the supervisor should discuss how he/she wants to use solutions from this case study as a way to change the culture and learning environment in the school or teacher education program so all teachers are reflecting on their practices.

The case of Mr. Gittleman and Principal Williamson was challenging because, on the surface, he was doing a great job. Students were engaged, learning content, and practicing different skills. The problem arose when Mr. Gittleman was asked to provide a rationale for what he was doing, or provide evidence of student performance.

Teachers need to understand that being asked to provide a rationale or evidence does not mean they are doing something wrong. It does not mean they need to change their practices. Often, teachers become very defensive when asked certain questions by their supervisor or colleagues. This is partially due to them proceeding through their professional careers and not being asked to do this (starting in teacher education).

Being asked to provide a rationale or evidence of teacher work should be common practice in all schools and teacher education programs. If it were common practice, it would reduce the risk of teachers becoming defensive. Instead, they will see those types of questions as a way to think through their planning, instruction, and student learning.

These questions cannot happen overnight. The supervisor must explain his/her own rationale for asking such questions and remind teachers that it is not a way to evaluate or judge their decisions. One way to encourage this is to have teachers ask these questions of one another during team meetings, planning sessions, and teaching mentoring. Creating an environment in which it is not just the supervisor asking a teacher, but common practice for all teachers to ask these questions, will help. In the case of Mr. Gittleman, his peers were frustrated. If it was in the culture of the school to ask these questions of one another, the relationships between Mr. Gittleman and his colleagues might have been better.

In this case, the supervisor might want to encourage Mr. Gittleman to participate in one of the combination approaches. Since he is a novice teacher and will be evaluated before he is tenured, it would be good to have him participate in a strategy that models an evaluation model.

Since Mr. Gittleman struggled to identify the skills students were developing and evidence of students' understanding, the supervisor might want to suggest the *Assessment Driven Lesson Plan* strategy (see chapter 4). This approach will give him evaluation experience, and it focuses on students' learning. This will develop Mr. Gittleman's ability to identify the skills and content being covered in a lesson and to collect evidence from students.

The challenge of this strategy is the time commitment. For it to be successful, a supervisor and teacher must agree to participate and understand the benefits of the strategy. Both parties also need to understand the time commitment that is needed during a very short period of time. If it is not a good time, the teacher or supervisor must feel comfortable asking to reschedule or find another strategy that works within both parties' time frame.

The supervisor should not wait until there is a problem to use this strategy. If he/she waits, the teachers will think they are being judged and will become defensive. Instead, this strategy should be incorporated as one form of feedback that all teachers will participate in at some point. Supervisors should also think about developing a school culture in which all teachers participate in both combination approaches to feedback as part of a teacher mentoring system.

CASE 4: PRINCIPALS ARE JUST TOO BUSY

Narrative

Principals are often busy, and juggling a range of school-related issues. Principal Roberts had the reputation of being a very hands-on principal. He was constantly walking around the school, visiting classrooms, talking to parents, and working with the teachers to develop school activities.

The school was a high-performing elementary school. Parents had high expectations, and the students and teachers rose to the expectations. Although Principal Roberts did not put pressure on his faculty about the tests, test scores were always high and parents seemed to be pleased.

Principal Roberts required a lot from his teachers and would constantly be in classrooms checking instructional practices. In terms of lesson plans, he required all teachers to submit their lesson plans on a weekly basis. He did not have time to review the plans, but he would have his secretary check to make sure all teachers submitted their plans for the week. He did not feel lesson plans represented what he saw in the classroom, and he did not want to burden his faculty with writing extensive plans. He would rather they put their efforts into classroom instruction. However, he did collect the lesson plans because it was school district policy.

Principal Roberts hired a new second-grade teacher, Miss Olive. Miss Olive had been a student teacher at his school the year before, and he was very impressed by her work. Students liked her, and she did a great job working with the other faculty. She had a lot of support from her college supervisor and cooperative teacher, and Principal Roberts thought she would be a great asset to the school.

During her first year, Principal Roberts would frequently visit her class. Students really loved her and seemed to be having a lot of fun. It seemed that students were constantly playing games and learning content through activities. She was a hard worker.

At the end of the school year the test scores came back. Her class was at the bottom, and 75 percent of the students in her class had regressed, according to the standardized test results. This had never happened during Principal Roberts's time at the school. Parents were furious, and they wanted to know what happened.

Parents of students entering the second grade became aware of the situation, and began making requests not to have Miss Olive. Parents had heard good things, but when they found out test scores significantly dropped, they were less concerned with how engaging she was and more concerned about having a teacher who could challenge and push their children further.

Principal Roberts did not know what happened. When he walked into her class, he was impressed, but for some reason, the engagement did not translate to student learning. He went back to review her lesson plans, and noticed the plans were skeletons. Her plans at the beginning of the year followed her college teacher-education-program format, but after the first two weeks they started to look similar to some of the schools' experienced teachers' plans. They did not have any information about content or how she would assess students' understanding throughout the lesson.

Principal Roberts believed Miss Olive had potential and thought some of this was due to being a novice teacher. However, if he would keep her on for the following school year, he had to come up with a plan. He did not want to construct a plan that would reprimand Miss Olive; he wanted to put a plan in action that would support her and develop her into a great teacher. He was unsure how to provide the right support and how to engage Miss Olive in a meaningful conversation about making changes.

Reflection

Before the supervisor and mentee have a conversation about Miss Olive and Principal Roberts, it is necessary for both parties to reflect on the narrative independently. Each person should reflect on the following questions before coming together for the discussion section. The reflection questions are designed to make the supervisor and mentee think about actions and solutions they would take if they were put in a similar situation.

Reflection Questions for the Supervisor

1. If you were Principal Roberts, what mistakes did you make in regard to helping Miss Olive during her first year as a teacher?
2. If you were Principal Roberts, what goals would you set for Miss Olive, and what specific activities would you want to see from Miss Olive over the next year as evidence that she is working toward those goals?

3. If you were Principal Roberts, what specific actions would you take to support Miss Olive in reaching her goals?

Reflection Questions for the Mentee

1. If you were Miss Olive, what specific teacher activities would you do to improve your practice?
2. Based on those activities, what specific forms of support would you need from Principal Roberts?
3. If you were Miss Olive, describe actions Principal Roberts might take that would make you feel that you were in trouble or being reprimanded for your students' low test scores and become turned off from having a good conversation about changes you want to make to improve your practice?
4. If you were Miss Olive, what specific activities could Principal Roberts do to open the doors of communication and make you want to engage in the process of changing your practice?

Discussion

To begin the discussion, the mentee should first share his/her responses to the reflection questions. As he/she shares, it is important that the supervisor listens and asks follow-up questions. This is not the time for the supervisor to share his/her opinion; it is a time to listen and learn about the mentee and the type of supervision to which he/she responds well.

Once the mentee has shared, the supervisor should recall what he/she heard the mentee say. Then the supervisor can share his/her responses to the reflection questions. As before, the mentee should listen and ask follow-up questions. It is important that the mentee understand how the supervisor viewed the story and how the supervisor would support a teacher in a similar situation. This could provide insight into the type of supervision the mentee would experience.

After both parties have shared, together they should give their opinions and feelings about Principal Roberts and Miss Olive. This should be an open dialog and a chance for both parties to connect and disagree on what happened in the scenario. It is important to be able to disagree on an opinion and still know that the conversation can continue.

Once the scenario has been vetted, both the supervisor and mentee should discuss the following two questions regarding lesson planning as a possible solution.

1. What specific strategies for providing lesson plan feedback could be used in this scenario?
2. What specific actions would each of you take to implement this lesson planning feedback strategy successfully?

Suggestions from the Author

This narrative was written from Principal Roberts's point of view. As the principal, he oversaw the education of all students in the school. To do this effectively, he visited classrooms and checked instructional practices. He worked to hire teachers who he thought would do a good job in the classroom and for the school community. Principal Roberts's support came from visiting classrooms and not through lesson planning; however, he did follow district policy and collected lesson plans from all teachers.

Principal Roberts held Miss Olive to the same high quality standards as his other teachers, and his support and mentoring were consistent with how he supported other teachers at the school, including experienced teachers. The problem was that Miss Olive was not an experienced teacher. Recognizing that teachers might need different types of support at different stages in their career is valuable.

A supervisor (principal, administrator, mentor teacher, teacher educator, etc.) will not be able to give all of his/her time to one teacher or one student teacher. It is necessary to identify what other aspects of the job take up time and be able to prioritize. However, a supervisor must recognize that the time given to a teacher, whether in person or not, is valuable and important for the growth of that teacher. A supervisor should work with the teacher to establish times to meet and establish how the supervisor will support the teacher. Establishing time that can be given is important for the success of the relationship.

In this type of situation, the supervisor might want to recommend using the *Lesson Plan Walk Through* feedback (see chapter 3). The strategy is designed to engage a novice teacher in conversation about the content and pedagogy before instruction. Oftentimes a novice teacher might be wrapped up in thinking of creative and fun methods for instruction and lose sight of the content. Walking through the lesson before teaching provides the teacher with a chance to describe clearly the content and methods being used to cover the content. This would be very beneficial for a teacher who focuses on the engagement but might lose sight of the content. The method would also work for a principal who could give time during school hours to talking directly with a teacher, without having to spend a lot of additional time reading lesson plans or providing written feedback.

UNDERSTANDING THE RELATIONSHIP

Supervisors must acknowledge that not all mentees will respond to the same type of supervision and feedback in the same manner. What works for one mentee might not work for another. A supervisor must share his/her approach, but also ask what works and does not work for that mentee. A good supervisor will be flexible and adapt his/her own style to align with the needs of a mentee.

At the same time, a mentee needs to remember that supervision is not about making friends. It is not about constantly giving praise. This type of supervision (lesson plan feedback) is about improving teacher practice and should be used as an educative tool. Mentees must go into this relationship wanting to improve and wanting to receive feedback that would challenge them to reflect on their teacher practice and make changes to improve their practice.

These cases are only four scenarios. They do not represent every situation or every type of supervisor and mentee. However, these four cases identify the importance and value in using lesson plan feedback. The different strategies for lesson plan feedback can improve a teacher's practice and develop professional relationships between supervisors and mentees.

REFERENCES

Ball, D. L., M. H. Thames, M.H., and G. Phelps. "Content Knowledge for Teaching, What Makes it Special?" *Journal of Teacher Education* 59, no 5 (2008): 389–407.

Fernandez, C., J. Cannon, J., and S. Chokshi. "A U.S.-Japan Lesson Study Collaboration Reveals Critical Lenses for Examining Practice." *Teaching and Teacher Education* 19, no 4 (2003): 171–85.

Gall, M. D., and K. A. Acheson. *Clinical Supervision and Teacher Development: Perservice and Inservice Applications*. Sixth Edition. Hoboken, NJ: John Wiley and Sons, 2011.

Garet, M. S., A. C. Porter, L. Desimone, B. F. Birman, and K. S. Yoon. "What Makes Professional Development Effective? Results From a National Sample of Teachers." *American Educational Research Journal* 38, no. 4 (2001): 915–45.

Grossman, P., and C. Thompson. "Learning From Curriculum Materials: Scaffolds for New Teachers?" *Teaching and Teacher Education* 24, (2008): 2014–26.

Hunter, M. *Enhancing Teaching.* New York: Macmillan College Publishing, 1994.

Johnson, A. P. "It's Time for Madeline Hunter to Go: A New Look at Lesson Plan Design." *Action in Teacher Education* 22, no. 1 (2000): 72–78.

Kagan, D. M., and D. J. Tippins, "The Evolution of Functional Lesson Plans among Twelve Elementary and Secondary Student Teachers." *The Elementary School Journal*. 92, no. 4 (1992): 477–89.

Lampert, M. *Teaching Problems and the Problems of Teaching*. New Haven, CT: Yale University Press, 2001.

Learning Mathematics for Teaching Project (2011). Measuring the Mathematical Quality of Instruction. *Journal for Mathematics Teacher Education 14* (1), 25–47.

Li, Y., X. Chen, and G. Kulm. "Mathematics Teachers' Practices and Thinking in Lesson Plan Development: A Case of Teaching Fraction Division." *ZDM* 41, no. 6 (2009): 717–31.

Lieberman, J. "Reinventing Teacher Professional Norms and Identities: The Role of Lesson Study and Learning Communities." *Professional Development in Education* 35, no 1 (2009): 83–99.

McCutcheon, G. "How Do Elementary School Teachers Plan? The Nature of Planning and Influences on it." *The Elementary School Journal* 81, no. 1 (1980): 4–23.

Remillard, J. T. "Can Curriculum Materials Support Teachers' Learning? Two Fourth-Grade Teachers' Use of a New Mathematics Text." *The Elementary School Journal* 100, no. 4 (2000): 331–50.

Shulman, L. S. "Those who Understand: Knowledge Growth in Teaching." *Educational Researcher* 15, no. 2 (1986): 4–14.

Shulman, L. S. "Knowledge and Teaching: Foundations of the New Reform." *Harvard Educational Review* 57, no. 1 (1987): 1–22.

Smith, M. S., V. Bill, and E. K. Hughes. "Thinking Through a Lesson: Successfully Implementing High-Level Tasks." *Mathematics Teaching in the Middle School* 14, no. 3 (2008): 7.

Stein, M. K., B. W. Grover, and M. Henningsen. "Building Student Capacity for Mathematical Thinking and Reasoning: An Analysis of Mathematical Tasks Used in Reform Classrooms." *American Educational Research Journal* 33, no. 2 (1996): 455–88.

Thornbury, S. "Lesson Art and Design." *ELT Journal* 51, no. 1 (1999): 4–11.

Van Schooneveld, J, "Understanding Teachers' Subject Matter Knowledge and Potential Patterns to Pedagogical Content Knowledge as Evident in Lesson Plan." (dissertation, 2014).

Wenglinsky, H. *How Teaching Matters: Bringing the Classroom Back into Discussions of Teacher Quality*. Princeton, NJ: Educational Testing Service, 2000.

Wood, D. R. "Professional Learning Communities: Teachers, Knowledge and Knowing." *Theory into Practice* 46, no. 4 (2007): 281–90.

Zahorik, J. A. "Teachers' Planning Models." *Educational Leadership* 22, no. 2 (1975): 134–39.

Zazkis, R., P. Liljedahl, and N. Sinclair. "Lesson Plays: Planning Teaching Versus Teaching Planning." *For the Learning of Mathematics* 29, no. 1 (2009): 40–47.

ABOUT THE AUTHOR

Jacqueline G. Van Schooneveld, EdD, is currently assistant professor in the Department of Early and Middle Grades Education at West Chester University. Her research has focused on instructional design practices and teacher practices that take place outside the class and potentially impact teachers' classroom instruction and student learning. Her experiences collaborating with teachers, students, administrators, and teacher educators and student teachers from diverse school communities have provided her a range of opportunities to support teachers' learning through instructional design practices.